Democracy's Little Self-Help Book

Peter Michaelson

Bloomington, IN

Milton Keynes, UK

AuthorHouse™
1663 Liberty Drive, Suite 200
Bloomington, IN 47403
www.authorhouse.com
Phone: 1-800-839-8640

AuthorHouse™ UK Ltd.
500 Avebury Boulevard
Central Milton Keynes, MK9 2BE
www.authorhouse.co.uk
Phone: 08001974150

This book is a work of non-fiction. Unless otherwise noted, the author and the publisher make no explicit guarantees as to the accuracy of the information contained in this book and in some cases, names of people and places have been altered to protect their privacy.

First published by AuthorHouse 01/11/06

ISBN: 1-4259-1218-4 (sc)

Printed in the United States of America
Bloomington, Indiana

This book is printed on acid-free paper.

Also by the Author

The Phantom of the Psyche: Freeing Ourself from Inner Passivity (2002)

Freedom From Self-Sabotage: The Intelligent Reader's Guide to Success and Self-Fulfillment (1999)

Secret Attachments: Exposing the Roots of Addictions and Compulsions (1993)

See Your Way to Self-Esteem: An In-Depth Study of the Causes and Cures of Low Self-Esteem (1993)

ACKNOWLEDGMENTS

I am greatly indebted to many friends and readers who have contributed patiently and generously to this book. They include Teresa Garland, Sara McIntosh, Madeline Stark, Pete Padilla, Derek Fowell, Susana Andrews, Michael Smith, Sheila Cowling, and Ralph Stone. A special *thank you* to Teresa for all her help with my websites. This book is dedicated to my children, my grand-children, and all my family far and wide.

Table of Contents

INTRODUCTION

This is our time to be heroes, when the tide of irrationality creeps higher upon our shores, as if civilization's polar caps are melting. In the post-9/11 world, as our government acts in a more arbitrary manner, those who are braver and more insightful shudder at the prospect of dropping liberty's torch. How can we live with ourselves if we allow people, driven by dark unconscious forces, to renege on the nation's destiny?

We are required, I believe, to produce something evolutionary to move ourselves and democracy forward. We certainly have the courage to raise the banner of freedom to a higher level. But something is missing. Our knowledge hasn't yet penetrated deeply enough. We have to understand the psychological undercurrents of conflict and disharmony, both in our own psyche and in the dynamics of society and politics.

Of course, much progress has been made and we have been advancing the spirit of the Enlightenment. But the feeling of our freedom and sovereignty can penetrate much deeper into our sense of self and reinvigorate our democracy. This book contends that our democracy requires a booster shot in the form of better intelligence—not the CIA cloak-and-dagger variety but the hidden knowledge in our psyche.

This new intelligence will produce a revolutionary freedom, on the scale of the freedom seized and secured by the country's founders, which will dramatically improve our political and social life. The country's founders established democracy in a great collective triumph. They had to fight not just the British but an even tougher opponent—the mentality of Old World class distinction and authoritarianism. Now our Lady of Liberty has become an old Raggedy-Ann, haggard from lack of attention and devotion. We have to fight again, this time to confront and understand ourselves. That does seem difficult, doesn't it, like fighting neighbors who abandon formation, slip on raccoon caps, hide behind trees, and snipe from the bushes. We are up against an old mentality too—the structure of Inner World oppression and authoritarianism hiding in our psyche. Our greater freedom means the overthrow of this inner structure, which is the next stage of self-determination.

At this point, a word about my expertise and objectivity is appropriate. I'm a former journalist who became a psychotherapist, and I write from an emotional and intellectual alignment with the liberal position. But I am not a political partisan. It is my responsibility as a health professional to present my opinions and ideas with knowledge, fairness, and a devotion to truth. I write as an authority on the deep unconscious mind (the psyche) because I have traveled extensively in those realms for more than twenty years, engaging in personal discovery and resolution. Now I clearly see many correlations between conflicts in our psyche and those in our social and political lives.

This book describes a learning path, suitable for the mental emphasis of Westerners, which involves the acquisition of in-depth knowledge about our psyche and the role it plays in shaping events. Most of us like to think we know all that is important to know about ourselves. Yet even the well-educated liberals and conservatives I encounter in my therapy practice are not aware of many of their own psychological processes, which include transference, projection, identification, displacement, denial, and resistance. Knowing how we practice these expressions of our inner life is vital, because the conflict, negativity, and passivity in our unconscious mind directly affect the health of our democracy. We need to eliminate this deep negativity to establish a more evolved sense of ourselves, and thereby exemplify the positive change that we want the nation and the world to embrace. This book gets under the skin of America's long-standing pragmatic culture to reveal hidden facts behind our common sense.

It feels now as if an earthquake has enlarged the divide between the right and the left wings. Right-wing leadership wants to subjugate us to the standards and precepts of some higher authority, whether secular or religious, that it claims to know and represent. Right-wing talk is about discipline, obedience, loyalty, punishment, and sexual morality. Listening to it feels like being lectured to by our parents. In contrast, liberals propose, as a first principle, that we are adults with minds of our own. We can't grow and feel free unless we can explore and discover what constitutes, for each of us, wise and unwise belief and conduct. Most of us are interested in acquiring a healthy self-regulation, but we want to discover it from within, not have it imposed from without. To do so we need, along with the wide open spaces of tolerance, the wisdom and strength that emerge from a deeper appreciation of ourselves. This connection to our goodness and value will inspire a fuller experience and expression of our sovereignty, which is a first priority for achieving our destiny in this age of increasingly sophisticated political manipulation and mind control.

The struggle against the forces of reaction can be onerous, and it can feel that the promise of enlightened times flickers far below the horizon. There can be some sadness and weariness that we have to struggle so to protect our country's values and our idealistic vision. Yet what can we do but honor ourselves as we deal patiently and resolutely with people who, as in the parable of the fox and the grapes, are unable to grasp our higher values and so disparage them.

The deepening of self-knowledge is one of democracy's guarantors. All politics is personal in the sense that social and national progress is the achievement of citizens who are becoming wiser, more compassionate, and more powerful in terms of self-regulation. Exercises that can help in this process of becoming freer and more powerful are provided in the Appendix.

1

The Atom and the Psyche

From my backyard at night I can see across the Rio Grande to the lights of Los Alamos. The shining city on the Pajarito Plateau sits under the Jemez Mountains of north-central New Mexico. Stored somewhere at that beautiful locale are 6,000 pounds of high-grade plutonium, enough perhaps to trigger a second Big Bang.

We need a big bang of sorts, an explosion of self-discovery that blasts away the fossilized paradigm that has us spinning inside pale shadows of ourselves. This big bang would split the psyche, or at least dissect it, and breach its well-defended exterior so we can enter and search for deeper truths about ourselves, our purpose, and our destiny.

It's not surprising that during the past 100 years the atom has been more accessible to human understanding than the psyche. We know a lot about nuclear reactions but not as much about human reactions. But it is human reactions—in ourselves, the family, community, nation, and world—that are demoralizing, sabotaging, and killing us.

It is a hallmark of self-sabotage (the behavior that accompanies our refusal to learn from our personal and collective history) that we get excited about something that has the potential to destroy us, while we are indifferent or even hostile to what is in our best interest.

Discoveries about the subatomic structure of matter and the applications of $E=MC^2$ arouse our pride, while knowledge of the psyche threatens it. I once saw in a magazine a 1950's photograph that showed three men posing in front of the controls of a just-activated nuclear reactor. One of the men gazed upon the controls with a radiantly triumphant expression, his face a luminous glow, his eyes lit up with kilowatts of pride. How intoxicating to create and control such power!

Carl Jung wrote a short book, published in 1957 and titled *The Undiscovered Self,* in which he pleaded for humanity to appreciate the vital importance of understanding the unconscious mind. In his view, the unconscious has been ignored "out of downright resistance to the mere possibility of there being a second psychic authority besides the ego. It seems a positive menace to the ego that its monarchy can be doubted." Jung added presciently, "Underestimation of the psychological factor is likely to take a bitter revenge."[1]

That bitter revenge is our march of folly, the path of self-sabotage that leads us deep into disharmony. Unresolved conflict in our psyche spills into the environment like radioactive sludge.

When we explore the psyche, we penetrate beyond common sense and access a level of intelligence that has been unconscious. We discover that we have more negativity than we thought—or would like to think. This negativity puts us at a disadvantage as keepers and cultivators of the democratic tradition.

Our psyche offers us an additional source of intelligence to that of reason and common sense. The word *intelligence,* often used in the context of national security, applies as well to the knowledge that we can extract from our psyche, which is a kind of council of vital intelligence. At this inner council we can begin to sit as a member and at some point preside as its leader. From another point of view, our psyche can be put under a figurative microscope and understood in terms of how it functions and how it influences behaviors and emotions. No wonder it's been called the engine of the soul!

Our psyche is a nonmaterial realm that the modern age has neglected, in part because neither science nor we as individuals can easily come to terms with its formlessness, obscurity, conundrums, paradoxes, and humbling revelations. Through the knowledge it discloses, we understand how our inner experience is contaminated by radioactive emotions and we begin to see how invested we are in maintaining this core of negative energy. We also understand how inner dynamics affect our politics and our democracy—and finance our folly—and we acquire more effectiveness as reformers because our self-doubt is being vaporized.

Our psyche is our friend if we know it but our adversary if we don't. In its defenses, denial, attachments, and resistance, it harbors the very elements that keep most of us chained to suffering and passivity. Yet it offers us a path to higher learning, the means to regulate our desires and impulses, and a key to a deeper experience of power and liberty.

At the gate of our psyche stands an ogre named Resistance who tries to scare us off. Resistance wants us to stay uninformed and ignorant. He tells us we are better off in the dark, that we will be too appalled and shocked to see all that subversive activity operating inside of us, beyond our awareness.

Indeed, those secrets of our psyche are well protected, and they do hinder our progress and well-being. Even when we are suffering miserably, we prefer—for the sake of our ego, identity, and self-image—to believe that we are in charge and know the score. This state of ignorance is a stage or a state in the process of our evolution. It's not mental-health treatment that most of us need, but new learning and insight about the inner arrangements that prevent us from accessing a deeper conviction of our personal worth, value, and sovereignty.

2

An Appeal to Liberals and Progressives to Understand the Psyche

Liberals and progressives have not understood the deeper nature of our entanglement with right-wing power. Democracy and tyranny have their counterparts in the human psyche. Our political and social struggles mirror the conflicts arrayed in our inner landscapes. Good and evil, freedom and oppression, justice and injustice, and triumph and failure are polarities of the inner and outer worlds.

We on the left are not innocent babes but co-conspirators in acting out with the right-wing a political conflict that simply mirrors an inner conflict. This inner conflict occurs between two psychological factions, one representing aggression and the other submission, and it persists in varying intensity as a universal condition in the human psyche.

The faction representing aggression is our inner critic, which is an illegitimate authority that rules in our psyche. The more we are influenced by it, the more easily we are manipulated and oppressed by social, economic, and political forces. We have not seen clearly enough the correlation between our inner critic and the persistence of right-wing power because seeing it exposes a dark secret: our willingness or compulsion to feel victimized and oppressed by powerful forces.

Thus the trouncing that we are taking from the political right is not simply due to our deficiencies in framing the debate or because of a billion-dollar right-wing propaganda machine. The right-wing juggernaut is modeled on the inner critic (superego or inner aggression), a psychological drive or energy that dominates our inner life.

This inner force is a negative energy or voice that is irrational and arbitrary. From its invisible perch in our psyche, our inner critic imposes its agenda. It holds us accountable and sets the terms for our lives. Its main interest is power and domination. When we don't feel our sovereignty with enough emotional conviction, we are in the clutches of this inner tyranny and unable to overthrow its rule.

Though it is a great limitation on our freedom, we take this inner arrangement for granted (if we are aware of it at all) in the same way that a helpless child accepts the rule of arbitrary, abusive parents or a passive citizen accepts the rule of corrupt, self-serving leaders.

A true revolutionary or evolutionary leap requires us to neutralize this cunning force within ourselves, as we concurrently neutralize its manifestation in the ideology and operating procedures of right-wing politics.

How does our inner critic get away with its demeaning and arbitrary authority? We fail to see the nature of, or even the existence of, our inner passivity. This is the faction in our psyche that represents submission. *Inner passivity* is the clinical term that explains why our belief in our sovereignty is not more fully developed. In other words, we don't feel our sovereignty deeply enough and act on it in the world because of our inner passivity. This term, taken from psychoanalysis, describes an important limitation in our human development. Inner passivity exists because, in significant measure, we identify with our unconscious or subordinate ego, which is passive or at best passive-aggressive in its relationship with the inner critic or superego.

Our democracy depends on more than just our effort on Election Day and our attention to current events. We need to become more evolved and well as involved, and available knowledge can speed the process. Our unresolved psychological issues create undesirable effects at the political level because what happens inside of us determines much of what happens outside. Our personal fears, confusion, dysfunction, and suffering are reflected in our politics, economics, and culture. Democracy's bane is the vote of citizens who, because of psychological immaturity, are unable to discern, let alone challenge, corrupt, inept, or secretive governments. When it comes to caring about our democracy, many of us, convinced for psychological reasons of our limited value, don't even consider being involved. Others consider it but feel either that their participation would be completely inconsequential or too meager for the effort. Our sense of value or sense of self has much to do not only with our political participation, but also with healthy, progressive involvement in life that leads to greater wisdom, compassion, and peace.

The weaker we are emotionally, the more we overrate the power of the right, not realizing it will crumble once its dysfunctional substructure has been exposed. We are led to believe that the power of the right justifies our sense of timidity or helplessness, when the deeper source of our hesitation is our fear or at least our own resistance in facing and assimilating vital inner knowledge.

Are we, then, not like the Prince of Denmark? Like Prince Hamlet, we are sovereign, if we can claim it. But like him we can't feel it. Hamlet's words, "To be, or not to be: that is the question," may be the most famous in world literature. The fame of these words and the fact they capture the essence of inner passivity are not coincidental. We liberals know the feeling. That universal condition waxes and wanes in our psyche. *To be or not to be* is the question to which inner passivity says *no* or at best *maybe*.

Consequently, whether in our personal affairs or as citizens we not only can doubt our value but we also can experience ambivalence, simultaneously feeling two conflicting emotions—affection and dislike—toward our own person. Under the weight of inner passivity democracy itself can become an obscure, remote, or waning ideal, just as the better person we hoped to become is perhaps a fading vision, a lost cause. *And what can I, little me, possibly do to help with national progress? How much of my comfort dare I sacrifice? How brave can I be? Greater involvement is too much to ask of me. Better people out there will save the day. I'll wait it out in the valley of ambivalence, try not to suffer too much, and hope for the best.*

How can we understand our predicament more completely? We can consider that widespread fear, anger, envy, and greed in our society are all glitches, bugs, or viruses in the democratic process. These unresolved negative emotions weaken us and take us out of the game—we are sufferers more so than citizens, individualists instead of an assembly, onlookers rather than participants.

When we feel our sovereignty, power accrues to us. The greatest power is not in guns or money but in our emotional convictions. Our greatest power, individually and collectively, is in our belief in our goodness and value. When we feel this, we are no longer afraid of having and exercising power, first because we no longer identify with the feeling of being victims of it and, second, because we trust ourselves more deeply to exercise this power wisely.

These times challenge us to open our minds, illuminate the dark recesses of our psyche, and see our ineffective reactions and unresolved issues. Liberals and progressives can be defeated and we could enter a dark age if we don't break new ground in our comprehension. We may need all of the love of self and country we can muster because we have our resistance and denial too.

3

The Greatest Human Achievement Can Happen—Right Now

Humanitarians in recent years have seriously considered how—through technology, finance, and international cooperation—we can end world poverty and hunger. Indeed, these are noble aspirations. Yet an even greater accomplishment is possible—the reduction of human negativity. Our negativity has been around since Cain murdered Abel. Given such endurance, we might not be able to eliminate it entirely, but human negativity can be dramatically lessened.

Religious authorities have tried to eradicate our negativity, which they identified as sin. On our behalf they offered up benedictions, petitions, and prayer, while humbly displaying in their own deviltry imperfection's upward reach. Their investigations uncovered the Seven Deadly Sins. These were rated in the 6th Century by Gregory the Great: Pride is really bad, envy less so, down through anger, sadness, avarice, gluttony, and—last and luckily least for legions of libertines—lust.

By the 13th Century theology had become more precise. Thomas Aquinas, known as the "angelic doctor," discovered that gluttony and lust (orality and sexuality) were very naughty too, and he declared that all of the seven sins were equally deadly. In those days religious authorities tortured and burned "heretics" and "witches." So the seven deadly sins didn't include the hate, revenge, cruelty, and violence that were administered to these "sinners," though the average heretic must have thought such cruelties to be more deadly than overeating.

In our day psychoanalysis claims that sins are symptoms of conflict in the human psyche. Through inner conflict, we each concoct our self-defeat, our recipe for disaster that usually poisons our circle of family and friends. In this secular interpretation, it's not so much about sin as about quality of life: Our unresolved negativity limits our capacity for happiness and brings on dire social and environmental problems.

Human negativity is a powerful component of our nature, and at any given moment we can color our experience in its stormy hues. Without always registering the inner choice we make, we begin to entertain and indulge in old unresolved emotions, which is our negative side and our dark embrace of it. This negativity of ours is the lingering ooze of our primal origins from which we can now cleanse ourselves.

(This claim to a psychological source for human negativity does not deny the influences of genetics, biochemistry, environment, diet, and culture on our behaviors and emotions. These influences can make us either more or less susceptible to our psychological dynamics.)

It's difficult to eliminate human negativity when mental-health experts can't agree on its causes and cures. Another obstacle is psychological and consists of the denial, resistance, defenses, and egotism found in the human psyche. Some "experts," among them proponents of positive psychology, believe that we need only to wear yellow smiley-faces.

No mask of deception can cover up the fact that we are negativity-generating machines. Yet we decline to lift the hood to see this power plant in our psyche, let alone start unscrewing its nuts and bolts for closer inspection. If we're willing to get our hands dirty we'll discover that:

1. Areas of our psyche are infused with negativity and have much more power in influencing our decisions and sabotaging our success than we want to believe.
2. We have unconscious resistance to accepting good and prosperity in our life and to becoming emotionally independent and more loving.
3. One aspect of human negativity is self-aggression, an inner critic or tyrant to which we are held accountable and to which we act defensively. We absorb this negativity and pass it along to others in the forms of disrespect, disapproval, criticism, hatred, and violence.
4. Another aspect of our negativity is inner passivity, which produces an unconscious alignment with being a victim and with feeling overwhelmed and ineffective. We are tempted to blame our reactions to this passivity on others, on parents, on society, or on biochemical imbalances and bad genes.
5. In our relationships and careers we can be compulsive about acting out our negativity, leading to a lack of emotional and behavioral self-regulation.

We can easily repeat self-defeating as well as self-destructive patterns of behavior throughout our lifetime.

6. We have, as the essence of our unconscious negativity, unresolved conflicts concerning deprival, refusal, control, criticism, rejection, and so on. We even provoke others in ways that enable us to act out with them the misery associated with this unresolved negativity.

7. We transfer onto others the expectation that they are directing toward us the forms of negativity that are unresolved in us, and we project onto others the negativity we refuse to see in ourselves.

If these seven points, call them the Seven Deadly Signs, received as much attention as the Seven Deadly Sins, human negativity—and with it terrorism, war, violence, selfishness, and fear—would soon run out of gas.

4

Our Psyche Chooses Our Political Coordinates

We like to think we adopt a political philosophy because that point of view is right. We don't want to consider that we often find our coordinates on the political spectrum based on emotional biases hidden in our psyche. Our political outlook often correlates with inner defenses that are hidden and complex.

Let's consider the psychology of some anarchists, civil libertarians, and antiauthoritarians. These individuals often believe that government is oppressive and ought not to regulate or control people. However they have, as one influence upon their outlook, an emotional bias of which they are unaware. They interpret, unconsciously and emotionally, the necessary laws and social obligations of good social order as unwarranted, excessive constraints upon their lives.

The psyches of such individuals is "bugged" with this emotional peculiarity: They look for the feeling of being controlled and then react in indignation and anger when they see attempts at control anywhere on the horizon or when they see anything that they can interpret as being controlling or restricting. Black-clad motorcycle buffs addicted to "the freedom of the open road" can have the same unresolved conflict.

The restraints of law and authority are necessary, of course; at this point in human evolution, many of us are incapable of the most basic self-regulation, especially when plunked down to live anonymously in large cities, without community cohesion and family accountability to moderate our desires and impulses. At some point we will likely be strong enough inwardly to handle total freedom wisely.

Radical militia groups, common in the 1990s, exhibit another variation on this emotional willingness to interpret situations through the feeling of being controlled. When these "freedom-fighters" rail against the government, they too are covering up their readiness to feel that the U.S. government is somehow oppressing them or is going to oppress them in the future. Or they imagine being pawns of a one-world government, their individuality crushed by alien regulators. Their tough-talk militancy, like macho posturing, is pseudo-aggressive, a phony bluster covering up their readiness to feel victimized and oppressed. For them, guns symbolize power, and though it is a shoddy, anti-social form of power, they take what they can get in their desperation to feel power. Take away their guns and even in a peaceful society they feel powerless, passive, and frustratingly anonymous.

People with an emotional readiness (or, as is the essence of inner passivity, a *secret willingness*) to feel constrained or restricted, are inclined either to be controlling of others (as a defense or cover-up) or passive to them—a harmonious middle ground eludes them. Many of them switch back and forth constantly between these two emotional positions.

Both liberals and conservatives can react to political debate not on the basis of the facts, but in the complicated terms of how, as children, we identified with our parents and their emotional issues. I suspect that power and powerlessness, rather than fairness, truth, or compassion, are the primary "frames" with which both the left and right identify and align. George Lakoff, author of *Don't Think of an Elephant! Know Your Values and Frame the Debate,* says liberals have been at a disadvantage because they think that people will respond rationally to the facts. Lakoff says that conservatives have been influencing people more effectively because they understand that every position has to be framed to accommodate our emotional biases.[2] Framing is the art of communicating with words and phrases that influence people emotionally, either for or against a particular policy or belief. Framing is important for communication but it has no relevance for personal transformation. It is not a substitute for the power of feeling and expressing our sovereignty.

The right wing exhibits what author Thomas Sowell calls "the constrained vision" of humankind, the belief that human nature is limited by the immutable infirmity of self-interest. This view holds little or no hope for fundamental improvement in our nature. The best choice, this vision contends, is to create a social and economic order of incentives, rewards, and punishments within that constraint.[3] This vision corresponds with the operations of the inner critic or inner aggression. This inner system of control and punishment operates with the evolutionary potential of a dinosaur. In itself it offers no possibility for positive transformation—it can only be neutralized. Its only "human" quality is a temporary pullback of its arbitrary influence and power, representing a dim flicker of "compassion" when its demands or requirements have been met. Thus doctrinaire conservatives, in their unconsciousness identification with the rigid inner critic, naturally doubt the possibility of the reform of human nature.

The left, representing what Sowell calls "the unconstrained vision," believes human nature can be improved. We liberals believe in evolution because we have known and felt its possibilities in our own inner progress. In our view, the search or struggle for truth and justice advances the human race, and the moral and intellectual *intention* to enhance the quality of human nature is a powerful force that has positive results. This is the left's ideal, but often the reality shows us reacting ineffectually and passive-aggressively to the right, while secretly expecting to continue experiencing the right wing as an oppressive force. This mirrors the position of inner passivity, through which we resist inner aggression by means of various defenses but fail to find the means to overthrow its illegitimate inner rule.

The following example appears to have no political context. But it illustrates that, while we liberals are trying to be good and compassionate, we can be failing to act appropriately, let alone with power and decisiveness. A client related an experience while visiting his family in a large city. With his mother, who was in her mid-eighties, and two sisters, he was walking along a busy city street to their vehicle when a man, apparently looking for a handout, approached them and asked if they knew where he could find work. One of the sisters, an avowed feminist and liberal, began to speak to the man, while my client escorted his mother and other sister across the busy street. There, still a few blocks from their vehicle, they waited on the sidewalk for more than ten minutes while the sister continued speaking to this stranger.

"I expected her to leave him and to join us right away," my client said. "The minutes passed, however, and she went on talking to this guy like he was some old friend. She had the keys to the car and we couldn't really go on without her. My elderly mother was tired, and all we could do was just stand there waiting. It was the last day of my visit, and I couldn't believe she was being so insensitive to us."

Finally, his sister crossed the street and joined them. "She told me the guy seemed so nice and she almost gave him fifty dollars," my client recalled. "Instead, she gave him two dollars and her phone number, telling him that if he really wanted work, she would find something for him to do around her place. I told her, 'He's probably just a con man.' She was suddenly defensive and offended, and replied, 'But what if it's true that he needs help?' I answered, 'You could have told him you were with your family, wished him luck, and just excused yourself.'"

My client had managed to contain his annoyance with his sister, but he remained puzzled about her behavior. "Your sister was afraid to show indifference to this man," I told him, "because she would be assailed by her inner critic. Her comment, 'What if it's true that he needs help?' is very revealing. Her inner critic would say, *How come you didn't help that person? That was very cruel of you. You're supposed to be so wise and enlightened. That man may really have needed your help. You claim to be a nice person, and look how badly you treated that man.* I agree with you that her first responsibility was to stay with the family and be considerate of your elderly mother.

"Your sister," I continued, "could also be identifying with the plight of this man. In her mind, he feels marginalized and discounted. Your sister possibly is unresolved with this feeling in herself, and so she would resonate in an unhealthy way with such a person."

In feeling compelled to be available to a stranger at an inopportune time, this woman also displayed characteristics of codependency. The codependent gives to needy people because he identifies with their helplessness and sense of failure. He discounts his own needs, feelings, ideas, and abilities because that is his unconscious negativity, to devalue himself. He gets his sense of value artificially, by being unreservedly available to others. This is a form of compulsive goodness and is far removed from an independent position of personal authority. Usually the codependent position backfires because those people to whom the codependent makes himself available will take him for granted or even disrespect him for his fawning attentions. He also finds it difficult to receive praise and recognition not because he is humble but because he doesn't believe in himself or connect with value in himself. He feels hurt or let down by the self-centeredness of others, but he gravitates to such people because he is willing to act out situations in which, through them, he is feeling (or being) devalued.

Liberals are often codependent, and our so-called compassion becomes suspect when it is based on the desire to use others to prop up our self-worth. It is humbling to consider that we are doing the right thing (caring about someone else) for the wrong reason (maintaining our self-image). We very much want to believe that we make our most basic life choices in the full light of awareness. We can be as reluctant as a fundamentalist or errant president to admit our self-deception. But all of us—right, left, and center—are misguided in many ways and fail to see the big picture when self-knowledge is lacking.

5

The Discord in the Liberal Psyche

In my therapy sessions, I tell clients the importance—in fact, the necessity—of neutralizing their inner critic. It's the quickest and surest way to establish inner peace and harmony.

The inner critic is, of course, that nagging voice we hear inside us that casts doubt on our actions and our value. I usually refer to it as inner aggression. Because of it, we find ourselves being defensive, quick to justify our actions, and anxious to give a good accounting of ourselves.

In my political writing, I tell my fellow liberals that this inner aggression is our foremost adversary. We have to neutralize it if we expect to overthrow, once and for all, the right-wing dysfunction thriving in America. The ideological right wing is a manifestation, a political offshoot, of the existence and mentality of inner aggression.

The ideological right wing expresses many of the characteristics of inner aggression, including irrationality, insensitivity, illegitimacy, protection of the status quo, and the desire for power for its own sake. This inner faction is stubborn and intransigent; it never admits wrong and never apologizes. It carries on in make-believe infallibility. It exaggerates the seriousness of situations and distorts the facts, freely administers accusations and punishments, and renders truth and justice subordinate to power.

When inner aggression goes undetected, or when we take its presence for granted as our "normal" unhappy condition, we live in the shadow of our birthright. We can't feel or realize our goodness, value, and personal authority. We are stranded in self-doubt and in danger of losing our autonomy.

This inner passivity of ours mirrors our nation's political plight where we, as indifferent or disengaged citizens, either feel helpless about, or take for granted, the usurpation of federal power and destruction of American democracy by a cadre of ideological, self-aggrandizing, power-hungry villains. Just throwing them out in the 2008 general election wouldn't be good enough. The Democrats we elect might remain passive and accountable to that right-wing mentality and agenda. We could be defeated in the next general election by an even more sinister gang of opportunists. If we evolve or grow psychologically, however, our democracy will be much more secure.

Liberal readers can easily agree with my thesis to this point. But now as the psychological knowledge goes deeper, they quail and run away. I contend that liberals, leftists, and progressives—in thought, word, and deed—are contaminated by inner passivity. We live with it and we live through it, as if it were a political straitjacket, a blindfold or a gag, or an albatross around our neck. Just as people on the right wing can think and act in the manner of the inner critic, so do liberals follow in the footsteps of inner passivity. But we can no longer afford this bitter deadlock of right (heartless) versus left (spineless).

Through the inner passivity induced by our identification with the subordinate ego, we can experience ourselves in a second-hand manner. We struggle with feelings of being overwhelmed, defensive, fearful, and victimized. We can feel and act, in terms of our citizenship responsibilities, as if our voice or vote is meaningless. This condition of inner passivity doesn't necessarily mean that we are weak or wimpy. Rather, it is the common condition of self-doubt, or the affliction of our non-being, through which we all plod under the weight of our uncertainties and fears, prior to the establishment of our more evolved self.

This inner passivity can create the impression that the course of our life just happens to us, as if we are children tagging along behind our parents. The more of this passivity we have lurking in our psyche, the more we allow its polarity, inner aggression, to barge into our life.

We are quite willing to experience ourselves in this state of inner passivity because doing so is easy—no effort is required, not even the effort of being aware that this condition limits us or even that it exists. Nonetheless, I must repeat, it is a condition out of which we can evolve quite rapidly.

Our inner aggression and our inner passivity engage in a dialectic of futility. An inner dialogue goes back and forth in an endless loop, inner aggression accusing and inner passivity defending. (Examples of such dialogue are provided further along in the text.) It's like watching, as one observer grimly noted, endless reruns of the old political TV talk-show *Crossfire.*

This dialectic of futility mirrors the partisan bickering in which Republicans and Democrats are now engaged, with the Democrats in retreat and confusion through the first five years of the George W. Bush presidency, displaying an embarrassing degree of self-doubt and passivity.

We have to be smarter than ever. We know that faulty or bad intelligence undermines our decisions and actions. To emerge victorious in the coming years, liberals need the best intelligence possible. Sure, the cloak-and-dagger CIA variety is okay but the secrets of our psyche are better.

6

Why Hating Freedom is the Passion of the Right

George W. Bush told the 2004 Republican National Convention that the terrorists "are fighting freedom with all their cunning and cruelty because freedom is their greatest fear—and they should be afraid because freedom is on the march." Little does our president know that he also is fighting freedom—*inner* freedom—with all his cunning and cruelty. And inner freedom is also his greatest fear.

In all of George Bush's talk about establishing freedom around the world, he assumes that freedom is complete at home. In his mind, freedom is set in stone, passed along by God like the Ten Commandments and America is its Mt. Sinai.

Those who struggle to grow—whether in our therapists' offices, lotus positions, or everyday efforts for dignity and justice—know that, while we are relatively free, our inner growth and the freedom that comes with it are not set in stone but are streams of infinite possibility.

The right wing has certainly tried in the past to crush our freedom. When the right chants its simplistic refrain, "The terrorists hate our freedom," this refrain rings true for them because they know what it is like to hate freedom. They know the negativity they feel toward those who demand greater freedom. They still hate the youth revolt of the 1960s, that historic (though somewhat reactive) expression of freedom and its aspirations. They hate feminists for the freedom to express their power and truth, and they hate gays for their sexual freedom. They hate the freedom to decide for ourselves whether to have an abortion, undergo euthanasia, or smoke marijuana for medical reasons.

The right wing hated African-Americans for daring to demand civil rights, and right wingers still suppress the struggle of organized labor and individual workers to have a decent life. They stifle and abuse their children for having minds of their own, as documented in their bestseller, *Dare to Discipline.*

Right wingers want to privatize all of American life because they hate the freedom of the commonwealth, the freedom and empowerment that comes from owning resources through the open range of our democracy rather than through the private preserve of capitalism. In March, 2005, they restricted another major freedom, the requirements whereby we can declare bankruptcy.

A reactionary fears not only social progress but, even more so, the accompanying requirement of inner progress. He refuses the call of the inner life, the process of change that eliminates our negativity and fear. America's current rulers, addicted to power and privilege, are satisfied to accept cunning for wisdom and an illusion of power for freedom. They do not want people to attain a higher level of freedom and the more evolved democracy it will produce. The establishment, as Norman Mailer says, is very afraid it will one day lose control of the American consciousness.

A die-hard reactionary resists progress because he or she is unwilling to work through the emotional discomfort or anxiety that such change brings up. He senses that some vital knowledge about himself is about to be discovered, but he makes a choice that such information is best keep secret, especially from himself.

In rejecting the challenge of inner growth, he must constantly protect himself from insight and awareness, and he does not want the people to have access to insightful news and information. To safeguard his inner secrets, he constantly needs to be reactive, vigilant, and bullying. He believes he wants freedom, but he mistakes freedom for the desire to go unchallenged and for his instinct to say *no* to self-knowledge.

He places himself in a closed system and limits his freedom of thought. In this self-imposed cocoon he takes comfort in the safety and the "certainty" of his perceptions. His certainty is mistaken for strength and his close-mindedness is disguised as self-confidence. His idea of freedom is to move successfully through life behind a wall of psychological defenses.

For all of us the process of self-examination is very humbling. We tremble at the portal of this process and turn away, in what Joseph Campbell termed "the refusal of the call." The humanistic psychologist Abraham Maslow wrote about our fear of inner freedom, which he termed the "Jonah complex." He said this fear of our own greatness, or this evasion of our destiny, is due in part to an instinctive fear that we are not strong enough to endure the intensity of peak experience. The Jonah complex, he wrote, is partly a fear "of being torn apart, of losing control, of being shattered and disintegrated, even of being killed by the experience." [4] With this fear, we become reactionaries ourselves, reacting to challenges by becoming passive, fearful, and easily intimidated.

The content of the unconscious mind, psychoanalysis tells us, contains elements of immaturity, pain, shame, passivity, and fear. Deep inside we resonate with many different negative, irrational impressions that we are not eager to expose or confront. We especially wish to avoid the humbling experience of discovering certain facts about our human nature. In particular, each of us is loathe to acknowledge how strongly we cling to unresolved conflict and negativity in our psyche.

We on the left are afraid of freedom when we cling to passivity, hopelessness, and feelings of being disrespected or not valued. Our anger or apathy are often the symptoms of our own indulgence in feeling dismissed, insignificant, and helpless, which are negative emotions unresolved from our childhood.

Liberals can resist freedom as much as people on the right. Of the liberals and conservatives I see in my practice I can never tell on the basis of political persuasion alone who among them will more quickly discover and assimilate the inner knowledge that speeds them toward greater happiness. Rather than a shift in political perspective, it is our dropping of inner negativity, which includes both inner passivity and inner aggression, that expands our sense of freedom, moves us from self-centeredness to graciousness and integrity, and makes our life more agreeable.

Human freedom is an evolving process that is experienced on an inner and outer level, although for most Americans the current paradigm emphasizes the outer level, as framed in the United States Constitution and the Bill of Rights. We understand freedom mainly on that outer level. On the inner level, however, a new order of freedom awaits us, freedom from negativity, which means freedom from fear, anger, hatred, worry, and passivity, as well as from behavioral and emotional problems.

Freedom is on the march, for sure, right here in America. Legions of us are becoming smarter and less superficial. The best knowledge—what we are brave enough to see in ourselves—guides our quest for personal authority and national destiny.

7

The Quality of our Fighting Spirit

Good, you are brave enough to assimilate the reality of the crisis facing us, the onslaught of misguided missiles that have struck Washington, D.C., destroying the architecture of American magnanimity and the foundations of our virtue.

If anger is the rallying force you need to denounce and dethrone these coneheads (escapees from old *Saturday Night Live* reruns), then take that energy and become a grant writer for Liberal Insurgents for Basic Sanity (LIBS).

Our dire plight might also inspire you to become a talkative patriot who strides into the fray with a soapbox and the Bill of Rights, verbalizing the next great chapter in American history, a spokesperson for the Liberators of Besieged Secularism (LOBS).

If talking or writing is not your genius, you can render your services from a star-spangled burst of options. The history of the revolution, as Bill Moyers says, is now up to you.

On whatever branch of Liberty's Tree you perch, your political success depends on the *quality* of your fighting spirit. By that is meant the expression of your integrity, graciousness, compassion, courage, good intentions and, of course, indomitable will.

Like the challenge facing our troops in Iraq, our fight is for the hearts and minds of the people. Our struggle for the soul of America is a war of liberation, in which we try to free our adversaries from the restrictions on their freedom imposed by their limited understanding of our union and the indivisibility of our congress.

We have to lead by example. How can we make the best impression? Let's start by understanding our foe. As mentioned, a basic difference between a liberal and a conservative is the belief of the former in the possibilities of transforming human nature and the conviction of the latter that such evolution is unrealistic. Ideological conservatives don't believe in evolution, in part because they're so blocked with their own inner progress. So we have to show them the values and benefits of human development. We can best do that through the quality of our fighting spirit. I'll set an example and stop calling them coneheads. (Dunderheads, a good dictionary word, is still in play, as is madmen.)

Elevating that quality of spirit requires a replay of the Boston Tea Party, where we throw overboard the dregs of our hatred, passivity, denial, and other forms of negativity. The way forward is to become more insightful and less reactive, more powerful and less negative. Then we become reformers in the truest sense—we have a positive influence on those we encounter.

Reactionary people may be enemies of freedom, but they are not our enemy. They represent the resistance to human evolvement that lurks in the psyche of us all. If we treat them as enemies, in the sense of having intense negative feelings toward them, we are only fighting against ourselves, as well as inducing more negative reactions from them.

If we are transferring or projecting bitter or hateful feelings on to these stubborn opponents, this is us at our worst. This is our lack of awareness as well as our own negativity. In this instance this negativity of ours at its source could be the still-unresolved memories or attachments of childhood—emotional issues such as feeling helpless, oppressed, disrespected, and ignored.

Reactionaries are just what we need. They energize us and act as a catalyst for humanity's forward progress. They present us with the choice to suffer or to grow. Like petty tyrants, they bring out the best or the worst in us.

Liberals as well as conservatives can produce negative, self-defeating *reactions* to given situations instead of wise *responses*. An example is the political correctness movement championed by the left. We can respond with disgust when jibes are made at someone's race, disability, or sexual preference. But that doesn't make it appropriate to start a political movement against name-calling. We overreact because we are willing to *identify* with the target of those remarks, thereby secretly sneaking into feelings of being rejected, disrespected, or devalued. We do this because such feelings are unresolved in us. We pretend we are having compassion for those being targeted, but we are covering up our own resonance with unresolved negativity in ourselves. So we are triggered and we overreact and we make a big fuss over political correctness. This attempt to impose so-called "correct values" on everyone is a distortion of liberalism. Seeing this imperfection in the quality of our engagement, the right wing is energized and fortifies its defenses against us.

The more astute we are, the more we *respond* rather than *react* to events. Reactionary behaviors and emotions are automatic, conditioned, and instinctive. Often they are defenses against a deeper understanding of ourselves and can be compulsive and self-defeating. In comparison, we are being conscious and wise when we *respond* to situations and events. Now graciousness and rationality guide our fighting spirit.

8

When Inner Passivity Pilots the Destiny of America

The source of the Mississippi River was finally discovered in 1832, after almost thirty years of unsuccessful attempts by different explorers. The maze of outstretched waterways in the river's upper regions had greatly complicated the search for the source of our continent's most fertile divide.

We haven't yet discovered (or agreed upon) the source of another divide, one that separates rather than connects us. A network of tributaries in this land of 10,000 social theories is hampering our attempt to track the source of corruption, power-grabbing, and militarism that is flooding the great plains of the American heartland. Millions of us, meanwhile, are watching from the shore as our paddle-wheeler, the Destiny of America, drifts toward the sands of reckless misadventure.

Upriver in the backwaters of our psyche, in uncharted swamplands of non-being where consciousness slumbers in infancy, the waters part and a muddy creature makes slow progress crawling up the bank. In a burst of becoming, it rises on two legs and staggers off into the forest.

Most people and many mental-health professionals are unaware of how strongly we know ourselves and identify with ourselves through this condition of non-being, our inner passivity. This mental and emotional identity causes us to represent ourselves inadequately, to fail to believe in ourselves, and even to abandon ourselves. This sense of self is often painful, though it is usually felt as a neutral numbness or mild dissociation. It is often our primary sense of self, and even psychologists are fooled by its masquerades of the self.

Inner passivity inhibits the expression of our higher human qualities of integrity, dignity, courage, compassion, and love. It causes us to fail to achieve (and perhaps even to imagine) our destiny. The existence of inner passivity blocks us from accessing feelings of power, value, and sovereignty. Literary critic Lionel Trilling described the essence of this inner condition when he said that inner development requires us "to retrieve the human spirit from its acquiescence in non-being."[5]

Through inner passivity we don't learn, or even care to learn, about the existence and irrationality of the inner critic and the inner authority it assumes. Correspondingly, we become indifferent to the liberties that governments and bureaucrats take with our democracy. The terms and principles of our democracy are negotiable, just as inner passivity negotiates away our inner freedom without consulting our self. Thanks to inner passivity, we are currently attending to the American ideal like bystanders at a mugging.

We grow up in feelings of passivity. As children, we are dependent on our parents or guardians and at their mercy. A child's passive experiences can include the "tragedy" of weaning, helplessness during handling and diaper changing, "enforced" sleep, and submission to rules and requirements surrounding toilet training and other socializations. Through childhood and adolescence we continue, usually appropriately so, to be held accountable to the authority of parents and adults. But the feeling is often interpreted emotionally as submission, and it remains unresolved in our psyche.

A man or woman who on the surface appears to be quite strong can be passive in subtle ways. Such a person could resist feeling vulnerable emotionally because it feels as if he or she will lose power or be swept into another's orbit. In the political sphere, people on the right wing can feel they will lose power, along with their sense of substance or separateness, if they become more compassionate, while people on the left can be afraid of power and hesitant to act on their own behalf because their inner critic, to which they are passive, will accuse them of being selfish or insensitive.

Seeing more of this passivity in himself, one client said, "I feel I'm a little kid running around inside of me." Another client, feeling she was making progress against her passivity, said, "I feel like I'm now standing on guard for myself." A witty client said, "I feel I live by invitation in a forest of assumptions that I take for granted."

In cases of people trapped in a severe inner passivity, their inner critic can become god-like when it is interpreted as the commanding voice of god or the devil. It has instructed passive, schizophrenic women to kill their children and psychotic men to shoot abortion doctors. Other passive people don't experience inner aggression as an intrusion—they are so used to it that it slips in beneath their radar, and gets all mixed in with the chaos of their mind and emotions.

Sometimes chronic "heavy thinking" produces an illusion of power, in compensation for inner passivity, but it can lead to fatigue, frustration, and even migraine headaches. Mental processing can feel like taking control and having power, but often it amounts to just "spinning our wheels." Sometimes people can become manic or hyperactive when facing tasks or projects, as a defense to fend off the inner critic: *I am not looking to be criticized or controlled. See how energized I am. I want to do these things and get them done right away.*

Inner passivity is a factor at all levels of mental functioning, and it sometimes contributes to learning disorders and illiteracy. It can also be a factor in obesity, which is usually caused by a lack of self-regulation with tasty, plentiful (though frequently unhealthy) food and an inability to protect one's health and vitality. Women can experience inner passivity as post-partum depression, when they feel overwhelmed by the requirements of mothering and the feeling of being burdened or enslaved by challenging new responsibilities.

Inner passivity also includes not knowing or not learning what is important to know about ourselves and our world. Knowledge is power and citizenship responsibilities require that we be well informed. Some people believe they are well-informed, but vital inner knowledge goes undetected. For instance, some expressions of passivity have a powerful sexual correlation that can be entirely unconscious, and the more that passivity is associated emotionally and unconsciously with sexual feelings, the more alluring it can be and the more of an obstacle it is to our inner growth.

Liberals need to be aware of how we can "libidinize" or "sexualize" our passivity, and thereby dissipate power. Classified ads for spanking, domination, and submission fantasies and practices frequently appear in liberal magazines. Such practices may be harmless enough if people are conscious of their inner passivity and the temptation to eroticize it. We want sexual openness and freedom, but not an expression of it that indulges the extreme of inner passivity known as masochism.

Politically, many citizens are erotically passive to power figures or celebrities in a way that is unconscious. Voters who are "turned on" or seduced by a candidate's personality and charisma, thus rendered passive and unconsciously liking it, often vote for a charming scoundrel over a less-flashy person of intelligence and integrity. One form of evil is the willing and eager submission of individuals and groups to charismatic psychopaths or villains. The psychopath's power is based on the willingness of people to come under his subversive influence. The "turn-on" for con men is often the feeling of power over their unwitting victims, while the victims themselves, when they slip into inner passivity, provide the shears for their own fleecing.

Gambling casinos, with their windowless and timeless environments, are set up to induce inner passivity. Those who profit from gambling know intuitively, through probably not in clinical language, that people operating from a passive stupor are more likely to act against their best interests. The allure of machine gambling is derived in part from the unconscious, emotional enticement of inner passivity. The desperate-to-win mania of some gamblers and their self-hatred in chronic losing are the wages of this flirtation with the psyche's dark side.

More young people, under the influence of TV and internet poker, are being seduced into gambling and are becoming fixated on it. Poker and other card games can be fun in moderation, but they harbor a covert danger: Because the card player is often completely at the mercy of the luck of the draw, he is confronted with an opportunity to experience deeply his unresolved inner passivity. However skilled a player, he sits helplessly awaiting the rendering of the deck. When losing, he passively endures the bad fortune of the cards. When winning, he can feel intoxicated with power and joy, and he is tempted to believe (as a defense against inner passivity) that he gives to himself, out of his own powers, the blessings of good fortune. Though hidden from his awareness, the compulsive gambler pursues not Lady Luck but the phantom of passivity. Gambling is the means he has discovered to act out unresolved inner passivity, and gambling is but a symptom of, or a means of acting out, his psychological and emotional love-affair with the feeling of helpless anticipation and even of being a loser.

Our interpretation of an innocent word such as *hope* is prey to inner passivity. A poem hung on the wall of my family's living-room when I was growing up. It was under glass, stitched in cloth in a frame, and included a scene of a sailing ship heading out to sea. Below the ship was written: *I watched my ship go out to sea / A store of hope in her hold / Some day she will come back to me / With a cargo of wealth untold.* As a youngster, I looked up at this poem a lot and felt some comfort from it. But now I see it differently, as a poem of passivity or at least as a verse that can be experienced through one's inner passivity. Such hope as that poem longingly lauds becomes a defense that covers up our willingness to experience in the present moment some sense of deprivation, want, or victimization: *I don't want to feel deprived or powerless—look how ardently I hope for better things and better times!* Rather than see this deep negativity, namely our secret indulgence in the feeling that something vital is missing in our life, we claim through the feeling of hope that we want to feel more connected and whole. In this forlorn condition, as we wait passively for our ship to come in, we fail to see or acknowledge until too late the cargo of wealth that was in our hold all along.

"Just as primitive man was helpless before natural forces, modern man is helpless before the social and economic forces created by himself," Erich Fromm wrote in *The Sane Society*.[6] We can indeed be helpless when we don't recognize our inner passivity and understand our affinity for the feeling of it. The solution is to expose this inner passivity through which our country's political dysfunction is made acceptable.

The collective effect of our inner passivity, even more so than our inner aggression, is piloting the destiny of America. As a collective we have difficulty being ahead of the curve and taking the steps, for instance, that protect future generations from deficits, depleted resources, and global warming. With inner passivity, we can't guide our nation in a healthy way any better than we can guide ourselves.

9

The Inner Politics of Pseudo-Patriotism

We all have underlying uncertainty about our significance or value. We compensate in various ways, sometimes with self-centeredness, egotism, narcissism, or claims about the sanctity of our individuality. In the case of the pseudo-patriot, his underlying self-doubt is covered up by national conceit.

If his country is perceived to be strong, this individual infers that he too is strong. If in his mind his country is the best, he recognizes this emotionally as a tribute to his own person. Of course, nothing is wrong with having powerful stirrings of national pride. When a countryman stands on the Olympic podium as the national anthem plays, our inner stirrings of pride and pleasure are appropriate.

But pseudo-patriotism arises from an inner hunger, the felt need to belong to something bigger and grander than oneself in order to compensate for how insignificant and unworthy one feels in one's own skin.

Europeans of the Middle Ages placed their allegiance in the blood of clan and the soil of territory. When those bonds were severed by changing culture, economics, and demographics, they sought a new sense of identity, and for many it was in allegiance to an emerging nation-state. What happens to such individuals when their nation-state drifts off course, perhaps choosing destructive or evil options? Those who blindly follow their leaders on such a course are, psychologically speaking, no better than gang members, people who are too weak to face the world on their own.

Blind allegiance makes them not true patriots but pseudo-patriots, meaning people who use their country, via identification, to get a feeling of power or of emotional connection that is missing in their relationship with themselves. They profess to love their country, but that "love" is contaminated. The euphoria or "love" of country that they experience is indeed a satisfying feeling, but it is a result of an inner defense in which the claim is made: *I'm not aligned with the feeling of being isolated, alone, and weak. Look how excited I get when I can join in the national fervor and feel at one with my country, which gives me what I want, a sense of power, connectedness, passion, and purpose.*

This defense covers up, of course, how much the person is indeed mired in self-doubt and aligned with feeling weak and insignificant. These pseudo-patriots feel great antipathy toward anyone who threatens their psychological cover-up. Feeling good and feeling right about their perceptions far outweigh any consideration these pseudo-patriots might have for truth, justice, or an evolved national destiny. Such patriotism becomes increasingly irrational. "In a country where values are collapsing," writes Norman Mailer, "patriotism becomes the handmaiden to totalitarianism."

The issue of criticism is also part of the pseudo-patriot's emotional baggage. He identifies with the nation's power and greatness, and he feels flawed and defective whenever flaws are identified in the nation, its government, or society. He feels that such criticism is a hostile act made with malicious intent. He himself is attached emotionally to feeling criticized, meaning that the feeling of criticism is a negative attachment in his psyche. Unconsciously, he denies through his defenses that he has such an attachment. By getting angry at those who are expressing dissent, he is covering up his own resonance with criticism and denying how much he is influenced by the malevolence of his inner critic.

As part of his cover-up, he takes criticism personally and reacts to it with indignation. Through indignation or anger, he declines to acknowledge his own resonance with the feeling of criticism. Even constructive criticism is felt by him to be inappropriate or wrong. Though the nation's democratic processes need vigilant self-scrutiny, he turns a blind eye to social or political flaws and corruption, just as his sensitivity to criticism makes him blind to his own inner corruption.

Some so-called patriots create a worldview that accommodates their conflict-ridden psyche. They establish their intellectual and emotional foundation on the conspiracies they see, the grudges they hold, and the oppression they feel. The last thing they want is harmony in their country or peace in the world because that would hold them accountable for their own lack of inner peace.

A true patriot is not triggered by hostile criticism of his country. He is passionately willing to defend his country from the threat of violence. But if faced with only verbal challenge, he can more easily, in the liberal spirit that makes America great, argue his heart out and, if still in stalemate, agree to disagree. This person displays wisdom and inner security.

10

Fear is a Favorite Form of Unnecessary Suffering

Fear is all around us now. It's not just terrorists causing it. World-shaking changes are happening and more are likely. Life is no longer so predictable.

Imagining the worst can generate a lot of fear. People often don't realize just how much fear and consequent suffering they generate by toying in their minds with the prospect of being helpless in some dire predicament. "There is no terror in the bang, only in the anticipation of it," said Alfred Hitchcock, the old master of horror movies.

We get jolted with that helpless feeling in horror movies or feel it as anxiety while watching suspense dramas on TV—where we identify with the actors in their helpless, out-of-control feelings. Immediately following 9/11, that feeling swept around the world like shockwaves. People identified with the helplessness and terror of the passengers in the hijacked airplanes and the trapped occupants of the Pentagon and the World Trade Center towers.

Helplessness is often an emotional attachment, meaning a feeling with which we unconsciously resonate. It easily produces feelings of anxiety, fear, and panic that are likely to be irrational. The more that unresolved helplessness lurks in our psyche, the more we can be terrorized. We also exaggerate the actual menace. In our politics, we are more likely to vote emotionally (for the politician with the jumpiest trigger-finger, for instance) rather than rationally.

Here's an example of how, through anticipation of helplessness, we can suffer long before the fact. An elderly man collapsed on the floor one morning while attempting to arise from bed. For several minutes he struggled to stand up before finally succeeding. It happened just that one time, he told me, and he was functioning normally in the days and weeks that followed. But now he lived in dread of a repeat experience. It wasn't that he was afraid of dying, he said. Rather, he was afraid of being helpless.

He knew I was a psychotherapist and he asked for my thoughts. "You're entangled in the painful feeling of being helpless and unable to manage your life." I told him. "Of course, it would be awful to become permanently helpless. But you face the prospect of experiencing much emotional suffering over that possibility before it ever happens, if it ever does. This anticipatory suffering is caused by your unresolved attachment to feeling helpless. It'll help you to acknowledge this negativity in your psyche—your inner temptation to experience yourself in a state of helplessness. As a defense, your fear says, *I don't want to feel helpless—look how fearful I am that it might happen.* If you can understand and apply this knowledge, you won't suffer needlessly."

His fear was emotionally (not reality) based because he felt it in the here-and-now as a chronic distress—when he was *not* helpless—before any actual helplessness occurred.

Millions of us do this on a daily basis when we imagine having, say, financial problems. Consistently doing so constitutes unnecessary suffering that can be eliminated with psychological insight.

Often the source of our fear is an inner voice or feeling that doubts, questions, or even denies our goodness. Mentally we can know that we are good and have value, but emotionally we are often in doubt. The more intensely a doubting or condemning part intrudes, the more self-doubt we have and the more anxiety and fear we feel.

The following exercise (not for the faint of heart) can help us to expose and eliminate some of our fear. This visualization exercise involves imagining oneself as a passenger in an airplane that has been hijacked by terrorists. No doubt millions if not billions of us have toyed in our mind with this prospect, but perhaps not in a way that lessens our fear.

The airplane in your imagination suddenly noses down and plunges toward earth in what feels like an irreversible dive. As a passenger, how fearful would you be? Of course, we would like to believe that, were it truly to happen, we would stay present to ourselves and take in our final breaths with some measure of dignity and equanimity. But many of us, overcome by the feeling of doom associated with acute helplessness, would panic and become consumed with fear.

Feel yourself strapped in the airplane seat and heading toward the ground. You have perhaps sixty seconds to live. Live out those sixty second in your mind. Feel that your life is ending. Observe your state of mind. Make an attempt to reach deep inside yourself to connect with some belief about your goodness and your value.

Transcend your helplessness by surrendering to it. Maybe you can sense that your consciousness will survive the crash, simply because of your goodness and your value. Perhaps you can feel that, because you wish to continue to be conscious of yourself and to appreciate existence more than ever, you have all the time in the world.

11

We the (Domesticated) People

PBS recently aired a *Frontline* documentary titled, "Is Wal-Mart Good for America?" This super-sized corporation—with its low wages, plastic merchandise, and passive workforce—represents an economic model that many people favor. (As I write at the end of 2005, activists in my hometown of Santa Fe, NM were fighting what looked like a losing battle to keep the corporation from building a second superstore here.)

This article, however, is not about Wal-Mart but about us and our passivity. Have we been swept up in an epidemic of passivity that puts us in danger of becoming a domesticated people?

Is our character, like our food and home products, becoming more artificial and less natural? The once-wild frontier is now a declining ecosystem, and the American character might be regressing to the same degree. The wild bears, wolves, and cougars are mostly gone, like our wild love of freedom.

It would, of course, be a tragic fate for people who encountered a wild frontier and implanted that wildness into the heartland of their character. What are some signs of encroaching passivity or domestication? They're big as the roadside billboards that mock our old wild spirit.

- The epidemic of obesity is our hearty acceptance of our invitation to the orgy of orality, which is hosted by the bioengineers of artificial taste and the corporate farmers of cornucopia. Who needs self-regulation when, in such passivity, we can experience life through the heightened awareness of a sack of potatoes?
- The Armageddon crowd, stuck at a childish level of development, is yearning to be saved by Jesus. Life leaves them feeling overwhelmed, helpless, and afraid of the devil. It's a mad scramble for the lifeboats, and women and children of the future be damned. These childish fears are symptoms of underlying passivity, and reveal the difficulty people have in growing up psychologically.
- Our addiction to consumption is undermining Yankee ingenuity. In a reversal of the Chinese Opium Wars, the Chinese, major holders of our debt through our balance-of-payments deficit, have become the profiteers and we the substance abusers (of trinkets and toys). As U.S. advertising ingenuity mesmerizes us, we can't stop being passive to our desire to fill our shopping carts, which, given the infantilism of the behavior, might be called our baby buggies.
- Cynicism and apathy are widespread emotional experiences that reveal our sense of powerlessness. Cynicism is a negative reaction to an underlying feeling that one is helpless to change or reform an

injustice or a corrupt situation, while apathy is, in part, another unsuccessful coping mechanism for this passive perception. Depression, exhaustion, and anxiety are also attributable in part to the passivity that lurks in our psyche.

- Television and video games can be experienced passively when they hinder us from becoming the heroes and heroines in the drama of our own life. Pornography, sports mania, and awe of celebrities are second-hand experiences of life. Emphasis on the military points to the desire to feel power, or to identify with power, which covers up an underlying emotional alignment with feelings of passivity.
- The widespread "entertainment" of gambling is a passive experience. We zone out at casinos and are fleeced there in sheep-like dissociation. We place ourselves at the mercy of fate with lotteries, internet gambling, sports gambling, and rigged stock markets, trading our dignity for snake eyes while exposing our skin to sharks.
- We stand around and watch science manipulate genes in our food supply and experiment with animal and human cloning. Misuse of the world's natural resources heralds a day of reckoning. The economy depends on machines and energy sources that pollute. World leaders seem unable to stop the growth of environmental problems. How passive does that make us feel? Perhaps we do sense a dire future, the way animals know of an approaching tsunami hours before. But we repress such instincts because they make us feel

> more helpless than ever on our little islands onto ourselves.

Democracy cannot withstand our domestication. Domesticated, we desire to have masters over us. Ian Buruma, writing on tyranny in *The New York Review of Books*, says that humans become the gods of worship when traditional gods are banned. Human nature, he adds, has a "wish to worship, to be sheltered by a great father, to bask in the reflected glory of war, to be mesmerized by the spectacle of power, or swept up in a collective emotion . . ."[7]

Is the rugged individualist going to participate in this domestication, this collective orgy of so what? what's the difference? never mind! forget it! who cares? *Surely not!* Yet . . . looking around . . . maybe so. Maybe we're not as different as we think from cows, horses, sheep, and pigs. No, what a horrid thought! How could I write those words! We have only to go back to the heartland, the interior country, a place inside of us, to feel the old thrill of freedom again, to understand what a dreary, pale substitute we have accepted, and to restore wildness to our spirit.

12

Overthrowing our Psyche's Right Wing

If liberals are willing to do battle on two fronts, the political and the psychological, we will quickly set the agenda for national progress. For many of us the psychological battle, where we have to overthrow the presumptuous rule of the inner critic, is the one we dread the most.

What does the inner critic have to do with political strategy and the struggle to keep and enhance our democracy?

As I have been saying, the inner critic is the inner intelligence from which the ideological or doctrinaire right wing acquires its perceptions, values, and manner of relating. Unconsciously, such right-wingers are mimicking the moods, mannerisms, and methodology of inner aggression. They are emotionally aligned with this major player in the psyche.

Meanwhile, liberals react to the right wing, its rhetoric and initiatives, in much the same way that, through our inner passivity, we react to inner aggression. The politics are very similar. Inner aggression has us on the run. It holds us accountable. It exercises an authority that is irrational and often cruel, to which we react—defensively, passively, and passive-aggressively—in ways that can be very self-defeating.

Inner aggression cares not for our well-being but only for the continuance of its power. Its rule constitutes an inner political tyranny, and so we harbor our own inbred dictator or tyrant. Figuratively, our inner critic is a dark-draped Machiavellian usurper lurking in the wings behind the puppet prince, our ego. This aggressive rule is arbitrary and illegitimate, but through inner passivity we decline to secure our rights and establish our authority.

While inner aggression is often heard as an inner voice, it can also be entirely unconscious. When unconscious, the clues to its existence consist of our self-doubt, inner defensiveness, and an anxiety and fear that have no obvious cause. In more extreme cases, when inner aggression is more virulent and our inner passivity more deep-rooted, we can experience phobias, panic attacks, and degrees of self-rejection, self-abandonment, and self-hatred. We also experience inner aggression psychosomatically, in our shoulders, jaw, and belly, usually without knowing the source of this tension.

I prefer in my writing not to emphasize the power of inner aggression. Instead, I believe it is more helpful for us to focus on our weak reaction to it, which I attribute to inner passivity. This passivity makes some degree and level of oppression feel normal to us, and it is an emotional center in our psyche with which we liberals tend to align. Our democracy, however, requires us to feel as free as possible. It complicates matters that we so often take what freedom we have to be complete in itself.

While it is more helpful to focus on inner passivity, we still need to understand the negative, aggressive energy of the inner critic. Why does this force exist in the first place? We are all born with *natural aggression*—our ancestors needed it to survive and so do we. Success and even survival require that we step assertively or aggressively out into the world to stake our claim. However, aggression is something of a Tasmanian devil, a wild, unruly force that is a problem for us from early childhood. A child facing an emotional challenge can be flooded with aggression. A child's temper tantrums, in part, are an attempt to expend the energy of aggression, to throw it out into the environment so his body can return to equilibrium. The aggression is substantial, even in the psyche of a child, and a child's weak musculature prevents him from expending it all outward. Yet it must nonetheless flow somewhere. So it gets turned around against him, and comes straight at his unconscious or subordinate ego, the center of inner passivity. The aggression accumulates in his psyche and, as early as three years of age, consolidates as inner aggression, an entrenched negative force.[8]

Ultimately, the force may have a positive purpose as a provocateur or agitator for evolution: Unlike other animals, we are prodded, poked, and pestered by it either to suffer under its tyranny or to evolve toward the self and personal authority.

The inner critic challenges our attempts to feel good about ourselves. A client said, "When I try to establish or to feel that I am a good person, an inner voice says, 'Prove it!' Then I find myself reciting a bunch of reasons why I believe I'm good, or have done the right thing, or deserve to feel good about myself. Sometimes that helps, but then the next day if not sooner I go through the same procedure again."

That voice that says "Prove it!" is both irrational and negative. Just the act of offering up "proofs" in our mind is defensive, and it lowers us to the level of that irrational inner aggression. If we continue to see this aggression as irrational and negative, and understand our passivity to it, we will feel a growing capacity to neutralize that voice or feeling without the need for defensive words. Instead, we will banish it with the knowledge of its irrationality and negativity and with the feeling of a deepening belief or faith in ourself. Inner aggression can be deterred temporarily by activities, distractions, humor, drugs, and defenses, but only knowledge, intelligence, and consciousness can overthrow its inner rule.

Inner aggression doesn't need felonies to indict us or even misdemeanors. It can pounce sarcastically on a wish or a fantasy: *Oh, so you want to get a college degree. This will be fun to watch, seeing you fail at this and making a fool of yourself.* Just our thinking about some innocent course of action can also prompt an accusation: *So you're thinking of going to that reception tonight. Look at you! You look disgusting! You really think anyone is going to want to talk to you.*

Our relationship with a critical or abusive person—in the form sometimes of a petty tyrant—mirrors the relationship we have with inner aggression. The more emotionally entangled we are with such a person, and the more painful such a relationship is, the more it reflects the inner conflict. Often we create acrimonious relationships because we are compelled to replay our inner dynamic in some external format.

Inner aggression often assails people for spending money, and the second-guessing of buyer's remorse is often due to such an attack. A typical accusation would claim we spent too much money, or didn't really need the item, or acted impulsively. We react with defensive thoughts: *The money was burning a hole in my pocket,* or *I've never been good at saving money.* Accusations about money can also herd us into the stock market: *Look at all the money those people are making, and you're on the sideline losing ground and being a chump.* We can be afraid of making our own investment decisions. One reason we turn our funds over to money managers is to have a better claim that any losses are *their* fault, not ours.

I had a tussle with my inner aggression when driving in town recently. I made a bit of a bold foray into a traffic intersection and the big diesel pickup truck that I cut off inched up to my open window and blasted its horn. Yes, thank you, point taken, I thought. My ears reverberated and my bones rattled as I swung out and headed down the road. Like another horn in my ear, my inner critic was now ready to blast away: *That was a dumb thing you just did! You were careless, even reckless! You're going to get yourself and others killed!*

I considered the possibility and produced this response: *I see you are trying to make a big fuss about this. I have filed away this incident as a learning experience. Meanwhile, you have no say in the matter. I will consider for myself my culpability and learn my lesson.* My refusal to be passive and become defensive with the inner critic calmed me down, and I soon quelled the inner grumbling. As well, I felt no negativity, whether guilt or anger, over the incident. I wasn't upset at myself or the other driver.

This is an example of an everyday sort of incident in which we can represent ourselves effectively and keep this aggression at bay.

Because the forces at play in our psyche are extrapolated into our social and political life, inner aggression also takes center stage in national politics. What we inhale we exhale so that the dogmatic assertions of this aggression are broadcast to the world as the harsh righteousness of the strident right wing. These right-wingers, who claim to be so all-knowing, have unwittingly allowed themselves to become clones of their own inner aggression. It's an alignment they unconsciously chose for the brute certainty and unyielding righteousness it provides. They live in fear of being drawn into the doubt and uncertainty of the other side where it feels they'll become lost to themselves.

Inner aggression is more primitive or less evolved than inner passivity. Survival, control, and power are the values it represents, and love, compassion, and truth are on the periphery of its province or range of experience. Inner aggression is intransigent, never admits wrong, never apologizes, and carries on in make-believe infallibility. Sometimes it gives us breathing space as long as, through our self-doubt, it has us cowed and cornered. This is the arrangement of a dictatorship, where the "citizens" are left unmolested, providing they are compliant and take the abuse or corruption for granted.

Meanwhile we liberals, in our inner passivity, are falling over ourselves admitting wrong and apologizing. If we extend this correlation to the family, we are the more intelligent brothers and sisters who stagger off to our bedrooms trying to make sense of the parental dysfunction to the jeers of our siblings who have aligned themselves with the parents' mentality.

This inner knowledge is a powerful tool for political and social progress. Liberals have been in the vanguard of human progress, but we now need a breakthrough in our understanding of ourselves and the forces that oppose us. The intelligence we gather from inner exploration can show us more clearly the nature of our relationship to ourselves, to the world, and to right-wing power. Once we understand the inner configuration, we are already changing and growing.

13

The Deeper Roots of Political Struggle

The battle between the left and right wings or the blue and red states is only secondarily about issues or values. It is foremost about the negativity and conflict operating in the human psyche.

We know how hot-tempered we can get talking about evolution, abortion, gay marriage, or disarmament. In addressing these and other topics we can easily react to the negativity that is unresolved in our own psyche. This negativity includes feeling helpless to express ourselves convincingly, fear of being undermined by the conviction of others or having to submit to their agenda, a sense that we need to be right to have substance or standing, the fear of looking foolish or stupid, and the impression that we are being disrespected or devalued by the challenge to our beliefs.

These negative impressions have to do with our psychology, not with the facts or the truth of the debate. But we are reluctant to see inwardly and acknowledge our unresolved negativity. So we take the easy way out. We convince ourselves that the negativity we are feeling is caused by the meanness or pig-headedness of those we oppose.

Negativity is a powerful component of human nature. The appeal of the negative explains why, for instance, politicians use negative advertising. It "works" (in getting people elected, not for making a better country) because so many voters, seeing or hearing negative advertising, are enthralled, though they are not conscious of why. The voice denouncing the political candidate is mirroring the self-criticism we hear every day, usually unconsciously, from our inner critic. Often these inner accusations are completely unjust because the "faults" being identified are often only our human limitations.

When we hear someone else—a political candidate, for instance—being described in the unsavory language of negative political advertising, we are able to deflect our own inner critic with the argument, *You see what a worthless rascal that person is. So why are you so hard on me? Back off and lighten up.* In order to make this argument effectively, that *at least I'm not as bad as that guy*, we feel required to vote against the rascal. Often, of course, having seen the negative ads from both camps, it's a tough choice as to which candidate is the worse reprobate.

When liberals, conservatives, or independents see and hear negative commercials attacking politicians, their own negativity is aroused. Even when the words of attack are lies, people are tempted unconsciously to experience the negative implications—that so-and-so is a fraud: *Trying to pull the wool over our eyes, is he? How dare he run for Congress in my district!*

Our baser instincts are aroused because that negativity is alive and well (clinically, *unwell*) in our psyche. The seduction of emotionalism prevails, and negative impressions can influence us quicker and more convincingly than insight or truth. Many people are unconsciously waiting to be swayed by a negative feeling in preference to a positive insight, especially if the negative impression "validates" their cynical outlook. Moreover, many people are anxious to relieve the tension of being unresolved or undecided, and they will take the shoddiest opportunities to relieve the tension.

Instead of being exposed, our negativity is being exploited. Financial interests are able to commercialize human negativity, as in the appeal and spread of right-wing media. The media serves up whatever trash draws a crowd, whose negativity is attracted to the harsh, ridiculing, and condemning tone and content of these broadcasts. Right-wing radio, writes Hendrik Hertzberg in *The New Yorker*, "is niche entertainment for the spiritually unattractive."[9]

Left-wing media is now growing in popularity, and the same psychological principles apply. The left tends to be more civil in debate, but our airwaves can be contaminated by the static of negativity whether the content is left or right wing.

The viewers and listeners of trash-talk media love to hear others being scorned and spited. They need convenient targets for their own considerable venom, and the political, social, or religious beliefs of others are seized upon by those looking for outlets for unconscious negativity. The same process is at play in racism. Now that hatred or scorn for African-Americans is no longer so culturally apropos as fifty years ago, unconscious individuals find replacements for their negative projections and transference, choosing gays, liberals, Muslims, and so on.

When radio and TV commentators rant and rave, the psyches of their listeners and viewers also engage in identification. The inner excitement is created because the program listener or viewer identifies unconsciously with the feeling of being on the receiving end of the verbal attack (which is his frequent experience vis-à-vis his own inner critic). Thus he feels a perverse pleasure in seeing someone else on the receiving end of this venom.

Reactionary people also make political reformers a target for their negativity. When on the receiving end of someone's bile, we reformers have to be at our best in order to remain positive or neutral. An effective statement to make in reply to abusive accusations is, "You are using me as a target for your negativity. I am simply representing a point of view. You are the one who is filled with anger or hate."

The lessening of human negativity is humanity's sublime labor. It is the best security in a world where weapons of mass destruction are science's robust, evolving spawn and terrorism the propagation of irrationality and negativity. As José Argüelles writes in *The Transformative Vision*, "We must begin to see that whatever else we may undertake in the near future, we must embark on the willed exploration of our own inner space." This is, he adds, "the evolutionary imperative."[10]

14

Bush's Supporters Can't Handle the Truth

Tens of millions of decent, honest, and hard-working people have twice voted for George W. Bush. Those of us who see Bush as an appallingly inept and dangerous president are pulling out our hair trying to figure out why he gets so much support from ordinary people.

The obvious explanations are that (1) these people are duped by words of mass deception, (2) they are voting against a liberal agenda that they believe undermines the nation's moral fiber, and (3) they are ultra-loyalists to the GOP. All of the above are true.

But deeper understanding is needed. People are not seeing how truly dysfunctional and corrupt the Bush circle is. If they did, many of them would withdraw their support.

So it's about the capacity or willingness to see the truth. We all know, to paraphrase one of Jack Nicholson's great movie quotes, that we can't handle the truth of our country's brutish side. So why is it so hard to see or handle this truth?

The answer is simple enough: People won't see this truth because they won't see the truth in themselves. So what is an example of this truth that Bush supporters are not seeing in themselves?

They are not recognizing their compulsion on an inner level that is often unconscious to doubt and belittle themselves. Many of them are rural people who experience much of life through the feeling of who is inferior and who is superior (a basis for racism, patriarchy, and authoritarianism.) They also relate to life through judgment of what is good, bad, permissible, and forbidden (a feature of fundamentalism). They believe (resentfully so) that cosmopolitan liberals see themselves as superior to them. Liberals, they are convinced, see them as backward and ignorant. So their unconscious dynamic with liberals is very personal, a battleground for right and wrong, hatred and retaliation. They retaliate and compensate by seeing liberals as their *moral* inferiors and by lashing out at their agenda.

In a process known as *transference*, people are compelled to perceive an attitude or judgment coming from someone else that corresponds with what they are prepared secretly to feel about themselves. Bush's supporters make of liberals a mirror, and in that mirror they see liberals looking back at them with the scorn that, deep down, these Bush supporters secretly feel about themselves. Heaven forbid that this secret of the psyche should become conscious! They have repressed and don't want to acknowledge that they have transferred their own inner negativity on to liberals. As a cover-up, they feel animosity toward liberals. In other words, the Bush supporter who despises or hates liberals is covering up how he is complicit in maintaining a negative impression of himself.

This shows how liberal negativity can make the situation worse. We must reduce or eliminate our negativity so that we will not to the same degree be targets of such transference. When we are giving off indications of our own negativity in the form of judgment and scorn toward others, we provoke the worst reactive behavior from them.

Projection is another psychological trick employed to evade the truth. Everyone has inner negativity, we liberals as much as anyone. Again, it's usually not something we're eager to acknowledge. Through *projection*, we cast off or displace our own negativity or shortcomings on to others, and we then get annoyed or angry at them when we "see" these faults in them. We do this through our preoccupations with political correctness, injustice collecting, and negative peeping (the latter two terms are discussed later). Targets for projection are chosen unconsciously. Sometimes we target others because their beliefs or behaviors clash with our worldview, other times simply because they are different. In racism, the racist "sees" in the other an "inferiority" that he, the racist, declines to acknowledge as an unresolved attachment in himself. A Bush supporter who "sees" in liberals the "evidence" of their corruption or sinfulness is projecting outward the judgment or condemnation that he is subjected to in his relationship with his inner critic. The greater his inner conflict, the more hatred he projects, the more he hates or at least opposes those upon whom he has projected.

Resistance is another psychological dynamic at play in our unwillingness to face the truth. When we access the courage to investigate truth and reality in our psyche, we encounter *resistance*, which is the feeling that, like reluctance to go to the dentist, we can hopefully put off for another month or two what we know needs immediate attention. Psychological resistance is based on the conviction that, when we approach our psyche for deeper understanding, we will uncover something that will cast us in a negative light. Often we believe (irrationally) that our "unworthiness" will be exposed. We can feel this way because, indeed, there are pockets of negativity and corruption hiding out in our psyche. So we repress important inner knowledge, cap it off with our anxiety or fear, and then tighten the screws by denying that such inner explorations have any value at all.

If we don't understand psychological dynamics such as resistance and transference, and if we decline to acknowledge the source of negativity in ourselves, we remain stuck at a dysfunctional or neurotic level. To see dysfunction in U.S. governance we need to have some openness to resolving issues in ourselves. Since democracy requires us to function at high levels of awareness, assimilation of this knowledge is vitally important.

Meanwhile, Bush supporters feel certain that he doesn't see them as inferior. With his failings and weaknesses, he is felt to be one of them. (Polling during the 2004 federal election campaign revealed that a high percentage of voters felt more comfortable with the idea of spending a social hour in the company of the folksy Bush in preference to the cultured John Kerry, in whose presence they would feel inferior.) Many of Bush's supporters know Bush as someone who shares their self-doubt, and they obligingly turn a blind eye to his blunders and incompetence. Since people who have similar emotional issues resonate with one another and support one another, they share his pain and support his presidency.

The Bush administration is dysfunctional and operates very defensively. Bush himself, with his negative attitude toward liberals and intellectuals, transfers onto them the expectation that they see him as an inept dimwit. Whether they do or not, Bush experiences this negative assumption because of his deep self-doubt, for which his stubborn certainty and militaristic adventurism are defenses. If this were not so, he would also be more confident about admitting error and leading a more open government.

Sometimes liberals can't handle the truth, either. When, for instance, Bill Clinton's autobiography, *My Life*, was published in 2004, he told Dan Rather of CBS News that he had sex with Monica Lewinsky "because I could." He said contritely that this was an indefensible reason, one he had to live with, and that he regretted having made that choice. This reason Clinton gives for having sex with Lewinsky is a defense, a claim to power. It would have been more accurate for him to have said that he had sex with her *not* because he *could* but because he *couldn't*—he couldn't say *no* to her aggressive sexuality. It is truer for Lewinsky to say she had sex with Clinton "because I could." Clinton's inner weakness prevented him from accessing the strength to protect himself, his office, his family, his party, and the nation from conduct that had so much potential for damage. Apparently Rather didn't see the "lie" that Clinton was telling himself, nor did most liberals.

When we live on the surface of ourselves, and only examine the meaning of our words, actions, and feelings in a superficial way, we won't examine that of our friends, relatives, or government leaders any more deeply. We can see deeper by working on ourselves psychologically, which is like appreciating ourselves as a work of art in progress. We are prepared to visit the truth in ourselves—and we expect to benefit in the process. We know that our country benefits, too, when we expose political truth.

15

Sex and the Right Wing

Fortunately, the mentality of the right wing is not set in fast-drying cement. Its viscosity is more like moonshine mash. With the correct insight, we can turn up the heat, distill the spirit, and enjoy the high of progressive politics.

The mentality that supports right-wing ideology is a many-faceted emotional and mental configuration that is largely unconscious and irrational. We have to be willing to examine certain tenets of psychoanalysis if we're going to debunk, destabilize, and distill our compatriots on the right.

Why, for instance, are those on the right so emotionally opposed to, shall we say, certain risqué matters relating to sex? Right-wingers, as we know, chastise forms of "moral deviance" such as abortion, homosexuality, gay marriage, and sex outside marriage. But their vision is blurred and speech slurred when corporate deviance—such as insider trading, fraudulent accounting, exorbitant pay to top executives, depletion of resources, and increased pollution—contaminates the commons.

While those on the right allow themselves to indulge many desires, especially for wealth, power, possessions, and status, they must, under the requirements of repression and hypocrisy, identify something that is forbidden. Often chosen for rebuke is the gall (or freedom) of those among the masses who think they are as good as them (or, God forbid, as in the case of us liberals, better).

Also chosen for rejection is the id and its chaotic energy. When we explore the human psyche, we encounter and engage what psychoanalysis calls our *id*, the primitive, rambunctious drive of unfettered indulgence and deviltry. The id is an actor in the psyche, a robust, rollicking, raunchy character, the thrill-seeking beast in us, the mad dog of self-interest, that all-night party-animal. Not surprisingly, some of its energy is fueled by the sex drive.

If we see our id objectively, without the usual gaggle of hang-ups, we accept its drive or energy as part of our nature. The more we evolve, the more we can, through sublimation, direct its energy into channels of creativity, joy, common purpose, and guilt-free pleasure.

However, people on the right, particularly "nice Christians" and their Jewish and Muslim counterparts, make an unconscious emotional association whereby the id is felt to be something bad or even evil. This happens because, bottled up with repression, these individuals have disowned (again unconsciously) some part of themselves that they are convinced is flawed, wrong, bad, or even evil.

What part is that going to be? Often it is our very essence, our sense of who we are, that is secretly rejected. In addition, people who are heavily repressed often feel uncomfortable, even shameful, about bodily functions such as elimination or the sex drive.

Now our inner critic, that grumpy poseur in our psyche, gets its cue and marches on stage. From its lips pours forth a rant of judgmental, condemning proclamations and commandments. Like a neurotic parent, it objects to anything deemed objectionable, including various forms of pleasure. The inner critic, flying the banner of its own self-styled authority, attacks at our weak point, wherever our guilt can be aroused, using all its fiendish tricks, including brandishing the Bible.

When armed with righteous dogma, it attacks our "X-raged" friends on the right, denouncing carnal knowledge as a forbidden apple or a hot potato. Our poor friends, who like us are biologically tethered to the sex drive, are slandered by their inner critic for a variety of sexual offenses including their orgasmic fantasies, wet dreams, and secret peeping at us libertines.

Like liberals, they also capitulate to the inner critic. Inner aggression doesn't care about our politics. It simply attacks at the point of our emotional hang-ups where we are weakest. Right-wingers unwittingly concede to sexual repression as an unconscious clampdown on unruly elements of their psyche, imprisoning their frolicking inner agitators, what George Orwell might have termed their "Ids for Barnyard Anarchy."

To hold their repression in place they become stubborn, acquisitive, uptight, rigid, and dogmatic, withholders of their own free pleasure (*anally-fixated*, as mental-health professionals are licensed to say). They want others to experience life through the same inhibitions, and so they are compelled, like William Bennett or Dan Quayle, to lecture and discipline society's members on matters relating to sex. Their moral certitude and finger-wagging crankiness reflect their urgency in repressing self-knowledge. That knowledge, which will reveal our commonality, is buried on scrolls in the Deep Psyche Sea.

Extreme right-wingers such as George W. Bush can also feel absolved of their repressed negativity by mercilessly incarcerating criminals (only the blue-collar-on-down variety). Criminals represent what they, in unconscious terror, fear in themselves—the loss of self-control, the takeover of the ego by "subversive" forces, the emergence of brutish impulses, and the acting out of forbidden fantasies.

The right's unconscious defenses in support of sexual repression are sometimes pseudo-reasonably couched, as when Robert Bork decries "the infatuation of modern liberalism with the individual's right to self-gratification," or when William Bennett says, in relation to sex, that Americans have adopted "a deeply ingrained philosophy that glorifies . . . freedom from constraint."

They need a divide between them and us to allow space for their negative projections. Liberal self-gratification in matters sexual (misdemeanors at worst) become a target of their projections, as they trick themselves into identifying us as the bad guys, while condoning their self-gratification at the trough of materialism (felonies at least).

Since they are the "good guys," they have to bank on it. They do not protest the uninhibited pursuit of wealth and power because that pursuit is their actual or imagined pathway to the crowning of their "superiority." So they feel entitled, for instance, to act the piggy at the trough of the national treasury, their "superiority" gorged at public expense.

Inner aggression doesn't zap us liberals so much in matters of sex (we're too chic for that), but watch out when we deny the panhandler a buck (*What! And you call yourself a nice person, you no-good cheapskate!*).

The sexual liberation of liberals is just one branch of our broader quest for inner liberation. What authentic liberals are trying to adopt is a philosophy, or a means of directly experiencing life that is free from psychological repression on the inner level and political repression on the outer. Obviously balance and moderation are important, but such balance (and its accompanying inner freedom and self-regulation) won't be found by cowering in a state of repression.

We liberals know that. We're not all bad. We have managed to beat back the superego somewhat and gained some freedom for ourselves and, through cultural liberation, for our right-wing friends too.

16

Rapture and the American Psyche

Millions of Americans, believers in the Rapture, are wishing fervently for the world to end. They would end the world to escape it, such is the pain of their psychological misery.

Their vision is deeply negative and basically neurotic. It stems from experiencing ourselves through our passive side, whereby we doubt our essential value or worth, feel overwhelmed by life's complexity and uncertainty, and are entangled in negative beliefs and impressions about ourselves.

Prophecy itself, when we are emotionally invested in it, takes power from us. That's because it leaves us feeling that a future is approaching which we are helpless to influence.

It is tempting to feel this helplessness because doing so is easy and effortless. Like children, we can remain in a state of passive trust and hope. This is why some of us are so literal in reading, say, the Book of Revelations. When we carry the emotional baggage of childhood, especially unresolved negative attachments, we are prone to relate emotionally, in an infantile manner to what we read and study or to the facts of life.

Our inner refusal to grow emotionally carries a price in fearfulness, self-doubt, depression, and passivity—the pain of psychological misery.

When we believe in ourselves and have cleared away enough inner negativity, we realize we are the creators of an evolving, improving life. We understand that we can each be a hero in the drama of our own life and the spirit of our own shooting star.

I remember back in the 1970s reading Hal Lindsay's *The Late Great Planet Earth* and being emotionally captivated by its powerful prophetic vision. I wondered, *Can this all be true?* I easily could have plunged deeper into the subject, but some instinct or intelligence helped me to reject the significance of the material. So I know from experience its emotional appeal.

The emotional seduction of the Rapture is unconscious and it goes like this:

> *Since Jesus will descend to save me, I don't have to be concerned that I'm not amounting to much and that I've forfeited a belief in myself. The inner voice that criticizes me can no longer assail me for my lack of direction and motivation. Now I can say, "What does it matter anyway? All my efforts are puny through no fault of mine." True, I can't believe in my self, but I can believe in Jesus. He loves me, and that's how I know my value. And, hey, I'm not interested in indulging the feeling that I'm a worthless non-entity. I want Jesus here, on my doorstep, right now, with my personal pass to His Kingdom. And I'm not wishing ill toward all those liberals, secularists,*

and whatnot who scorn me and my belief. It's Jesus who knows who and what is good or bad, and He's the one who will destroy those who've rejected Him.

The apocalyptic conviction that the world is filled with evil creates the impression that political negotiation or diplomacy is futile. The more "evil" we "see" in the world, the deeper the state of passivity we can induce. The black-and-white feeling is:

Even Jesus can't talk to those lost souls. Better to withdraw and shun or reject the world, or else we'll have to destroy that evil through force, meaning we must build up our military and keep open the nuclear option.

This is a projection on to others of one's own intransigence, meaning one's own unwillingness to see and clear away inner negativity: *They're the ones who refuse to change, not me.*

President Bush must be under the spell of the Rapture because he has concocted a foreign policy that mimics it. He believes in combative intervention (in the Middle East), a model based on Jesus coming to save some of us and allowing the rest of us to be destroyed (as in the Great Tribulation). Believing in salvation, Bush "saves" the people of Iraq, delivering them from evil, while allowing many to be destroyed.

The secular option is less passive than the fundamentalist one. The secular choice is an expression of our belief in ourselves. It says, "We can be stewards in our own domain. This earth is our domain, and we are grateful for the opportunity to discover and to express our very best. Let's see what we're made of!"

We secularists are inwardly braver than those escapists, so we want the chance, as in Star Trek's non-intervention philosophy, to do our thing without interference from on high. Otherwise, it's like a parent always telling us how to do something, when the greater satisfaction is often in learning or discovering for ourselves.

The Rapture ought to be called the Rupture. It is like taking a butcher knife to our destiny and hacking at it like a fiend. Who would do that other than someone too afraid to face himself?

17

How Religion is Misused to Deflect Our Inner Critic

Those religious people who in America have entered the political fray with the intention of breaching the church-state divide and canonizing the law must now, to be fair and balanced, allow their beliefs to be scrutinized while showing some spunk by not reacting irrationally.

Many religious people feel attacked when their beliefs are examined analytically. Feeling attacked, they attack back, accusing the scrutinizer of being, at best, a disbeliever, detractor, or bigot; at worst, he is deemed to be, as in Salman Rushdie's case, a denigrator worthy of assassination.

Not many politicians or media outlets, thinking of votes or boycotts, are going to put the fervor of the Christian Coalition under a microscope. But independent writers and commentators care about the truth and make it their business to put emotionally challenging ideas out for debate.

Negative reactions to attempts at objective scrutiny occur when religious beliefs are held mostly for emotional purposes (as is often the case). The believer reacts to protect himself (rather than to protect the truth) from the anxiety he feels when his world view is threatened.

The claim of some traditions in Judeo-Christianity that we are inherently wicked represents the position of the inner critic. "The wrath of God" is the wrath of the inner critic. Religious leaders devised the concept of Original Sin, which may express an intuitive knowing that darkness or negativity dwells inside of us. We had fallen from grace, it was taught, and thus we needed to be saved or redeemed. We used the love of God or at least the promise of salvation as an antidote to the wicked and vicious judgments of the inner critic.

In this traditional religious model God holds us accountable, rules over us, and demands our subservience and obedience. We, in our self-doubt, resist or conform; black sheep or white, we're sheep either way. This reflects the arrangement favored by the inner critic, that whether we are "bad criminals" or "good citizens" we are nonetheless reactive to it and under its influence.

Thus many religions have externalized our inner predicament. Instead of saying that we live in the shadow of ourself at the mercy of the inner critic, their theologies claimed that we live in the shadow of God, at the mercy of his judgment. As many religious leaders still see it, humanity is caught between God's condemnation and his mercy. This mirrors the inner dynamic that exists between inner aggression and inner passivity, where the former condemns and the latter maneuvers for mercy.

Freedom in the traditional religious model is the state of Holy Grace, where through persistent, saintly effort we rise above our worldly condition and become free of sin. In my psychological model, which in particular seeks to resolve the conflict between inner passivity and inner aggression, freedom means liberation from the conflict and its negativity. Thus freed, we merge with our self, our inner temple of higher reason and evolved attributes, where our suffering is much reduced and we can implant in society our growing humanity. This inner independence was and still is in many quarters considered a state of heresy, a vile assumption of devil's pride, a false claim of godliness, much worse than being a black sheep. This claim is particularly infuriating to people who live in the shadow of their self, trapped in a psychological condition of self-doubt and inner abuse while waiting passively to be saved.

The inner critic exercises its power over us in either a religious or a secular language, depending on our belief system. It doesn't care what language we react to, as long as we are held in its thrall. One client, for example, felt shame that he had twice been married and divorced; he was embarrassed when new friends found this out. The language of his inner critic was secular—he was inwardly accused of stupidity and failure, not of sinfulness. The more his inner passivity allowed his lack of marital success to be used as a pretext for accusations of failure, the more shame and embarrassment he felt. Now, as a result of his growing insight, he was learning the positive, liberated alternative—to uncover vital knowledge from his mistakes, to strive to understand his role in these dysfunctional relationships, and to block his inner critic's attempts to "pile on" with sarcasm and derision.

A psychological "sin" of the pseudo-religious is their use of God to protect themselves from their fear of inner aggression. God is handy and conveniently provides an excellent cover: *In embracing God, I'm being good and doing good. That makes me feel more secure. And I don't have to address my own negativity and fears. This is much easier than facing myself and uncovering the negative source in myself. And under the cover of religion, I can get very indignant and accuse of mean-spiritedness, hatred, and blasphemy anyone who challenges this arrangement.*

God is being used for the purpose of reducing the suffering of a hateful relationship with oneself. The *Jesus Loves You* slogan is medicine that many take to anesthetize unconscious negativity. The resulting fervor for Jesus in such a case is not love for him but emotional dependency. "Love objects" are similarly used in romantic relationships in order to feel better about oneself: *Look at how much that person admires me, even loves me. That shows I must be good and have value.* Often the initial "high" of falling in love is based in part on how the other person's initial admiration (while the honeymoon lasts) neutralizes our inner critic.

Because of inner aggression we face the agony *not* of actually being a solitary, inconsequential non-entity, but of *feeling ourselves to be* such a creature. In order to present evidence of our value to demeaning inner aggression, we seize upon egotism, narcissism, conquest, and control, and stock our trophy-case with worldly exhibits, to secure and establish our standing in the universe. But our nervous and often frantic efforts to avoid the negative accusations are themselves reactionary as well as self-defeating.

People who obsess over ethics and morality lack confidence in their own authority. Inner aggression challenges their choices, and torments them with impressions of being wrong or bad. In order to neutralize it, they need to have a "right" choice and a "wrong" choice. They can't be assailed as easily if they can demonstrate the blood, sweat, and tears that went into making the "right" choice. Of course, in so many instances, one choice or the other is okay; given two or more choices, we can often make any one of them work. Nevertheless, some people become lost emotionally in the self-imposed complexity of moral dilemmas, and become peons to be led by others into "the light."

Because of inner aggression, our attempts to feel free can feel reckless and irresponsible. Inner aggression fiercely objects to our "presumption" that we can live without its interference or oversight. Often, through it, we speak to ourselves, inwardly with harshness rather than sensitivity, questioning and challenging our belief in ourself.

When this dark force is neutralized, religious belief becomes a secondary concern. Our primary concern, which now feels natural, is to treat others with the respect and graciousness that we feel toward ourself.

18

The Religion of Liberals

Liberals believe conservatives are close-minded, dogmatic, hide-bound, and reactionary. We liberals are especially appalled by conservative ideologues we see passing through life wearing blinders at the bottom of a deep rut on the low road back to the Dark Ages.

Liberals, however, also have a religion which, like grand inquisitors clutching red-hot tongs, we brandish in the face of reality. I'm referring to the Doctrine of Innocence, an edict passed some centuries ago in the liberal psyche, which decrees that the devil in others causes the bad things that happen to us.

As it turns out, the DOI (Doctrine of Innocence) is a DWI (dead-wrong ideology). Because of it liberals are navigating through life as if DUI (driving under the influence). The DOI divides the world into victims and victimizers. According to liberal credo, the world's great problem—social injustice—is caused by the greed, cruelty, ignorance, fear, and stupidity of victimizers. All would be well, liberals like to believe, if we could depose those Republican tyrants.

The DOI decrees that Freud and his overheated cigar were just blowing smoke with that talk about the superego, the death instinct, and the repetition compulsion. Liberals want to believe we are innocent babes corrupted by the cruelty of oppressors, rather than complex creatures with a negative, destructive force at play in our psyche. Not even *Star Wars* and its account of the Force and the Dark Side can shake our faith in our purity.

When liberals say, "The devil made me do it," we mean the devils in the GOP. When liberals say, "Inner demons got me down," we are referring to the spooks at the CIA.

Liberals and leftists often seem convinced that economic and social reform can be achieved exclusively through the application of enlightened external measures involving the law, increased citizen participation, and cultural norms. People on the right, in comparison, have a truer sense of the dark side of human nature and correctly accentuate the importance of personal responsibility and accountability in achieving personal and social progress.

The good, bad, and ugly permeate all life. Positive and negative energies, along with plus and minus values, exist in all natural systems. Dark and light, night and day, death and life are unavoidable. Good and evil give vigor to our religions and joy and sorrow to our passions. Human negativity is born and bred in our psyche, along with mystery, complexity, greatness, and (my guess) immortality. What is wrong with admitting that? What is wrong with being a hero like Luke Skywalker and defeating the enemy within? When enough of us do that, dysfunctional government will disappear.

We each have an inner domain to govern, and it is our task to consolidate therein a reign of inner harmony, personal authority, and personal responsibility, thereby planting democracy in the soil of our being.

Recently the conservative *New York Times* columnist, David Brooks, wrote, "If I were a liberal, I'd argue about human nature and the American character." He is pointing liberals in a good direction. To be more specific he might have said, "If I were a liberal, I'd try to understand human nature more fully in order to see what can be done to ennoble myself and the American character."

19

Humor Lacks Punch as a Tool of Reform

Hail to humorists! These witty phrasemongers of the ironic, the droll, and the absurd can, with the lash of a tongue or the swipe of a mouse, mock the pompous, lampoon the hypocrites, and twit the terrible. If only more of them would write self-help books.

Here's a partial honor-roll: Mark Twain, Garrison Keillor, Benjamin Franklin, Calvin Trillin, Michael Moore, Molly Ivins, Al Franken, and Russell Baker—good writers and good liberals all, though Franklin, for the Good of the Publick, played no favorites. The Founding Father did write our first self-help book, a series of almanacs in which Poor Richard in the mid-1700s extols the virtues of self-regulation, which shows that therapy cometh before the Revolution.

Humor, of course, is a human capacity or talent for which we are all extremely grateful. But it is not sacrosanct, despite Jay Leno's Holy-Moses salary. Humor can be dissected by the nimble-minded analyst, who, though driven to find out why he still yearns to be a stand-up comic despite a missing funny-bone, yearns still more to be objective.

Humor and comedy have an interesting underbelly that when tickled registers no laughs. Humor is often an expression of self-doubt and a method of repression, which means it lacks punch when it comes to overthrowing tyranny. The person who becomes a comedian has likely made a fine art of deflecting or neutralizing inner attacks by reducing them to absurdity. Such humor is used defensively. Because he practices inner protection through his wit, irony, and sarcasm, his verbal adroitness in this format carries over to his persona and can make him a star comic or at least a sparkling personality. While he can deflect or confound the inner critic and the outer tyrant and even mock them, he can't overthrow them. The court jester, often a specialist at self-preservation, is no threat to the king.

Liberals often use humor in scorning, ridiculing, and mocking the antics of the powerful. Such humor provides a cover for jabbing at authority, but leaves authoritarian systems and psychopathic corporations laughing with the SEC and the FCC all the way to Fort Knox. Such humor is too reactive and, as a hit-and-run passive-aggressive style of skirmishing, outmaneuvered and outgunned.

Some of us have a more menacing or vicious experience of our inner critic, as well as a larger dose of inner passivity, than do others. Comedians or class clowns became very adept from a young age at reducing to absurdity the content of those inner attacks or the precepts of that authority. The humorist often presents "artificial victims" to his inner critic (his jokes often describe bunglers who make fools of themselves) as substitutes for himself. Another variation is to make of oneself a fool or an object of ridicule—the Rodney Dangerfield self-derision persona. He gets a laugh (as well as validation for his comic skill) because people are happy to see someone other than themselves—the victim who parodies himself—dangling on the butt-end of the joke. This applies, too, to the "insult comedy" of Don Rickles and the "big oaf" persona of Jackie Gleason. Gossip of the derogatory variety also serves this purpose of choosing a derided victim as our sacrifice to inner aggression. The fool of the Dumb and Dumber genre plays an important role in lightening our psychological burden: *Mock on, mock on, wicked inner malinger—slander yon exhibitionistic whiner; And I will laugh with glee—that a laughingstock diverted thee.*

No inner growth occurs, however, when we cackle so. Our burden has been lightened only temporarily. Soon our inner critic swings its hatchet back on us. Humor as a form of defending ourselves from the inner critic is passive and unstable. It's like playing chess against a supercomputer—one nervous twitch and we're done. Many famous comedians have died young from self-abuse or have committed suicide because their inner conflict was so intense.

We can take solace in the fact that liberal humor is greatly superior to conservative humor. We have a lot of practice passive-aggressively jabbing and poking at the inner critic as we resist its influence, while conservatives are more respectful of this inner authority and more likely to identify with it.

My hometown newspaper, *The New Mexican*, runs daily, side-by-side at the bottom of its editorial page, a conservative comic-strip (Mallard Fillmore) and a liberal one (Doonesbury). The paper often gets letters to the editor begging to have the Fillmore cartoon terminated, arguing that the right-wing mallard is the laughingstock of the Comedy Guild. Don't terminate the strip! It's motivational: If this is conservative humor, we'll man the ramparts to save liberalism.

Conservative humor is rather old-fashioned, like cannonballs of cynicism fired off by the gunpowder of sarcasm. Ignited by cannoneers like Rush Limbaugh et al, this "humor" consists of derogatory scatter-shot registering high collateral damage. Though duds they still ignite on impact and set afire the simmering egos of angry white men, setting off sparks among their women and children that torch family harmony.

This kind of humor fires up people who'd sooner fight than laugh. So our clash of convictions is no laughing-matter.

20

Weak Leaders Substitute Control for Governance

It is no surprise that the Patriot Act, a seizure of power and control at the expense of our freedom, was enacted at a moment of fear and weakness. Our leaders felt overwhelmed, bewildered, and defensive immediately following 9/11. Their idea of being in control was to restrict our freedom.

Doing that to us wasn't such a big concern to them. Their main interest was to avoid the unpleasant, often panicky feeling of *not* being in control.

The weaker the political leader, the more his or her idea of power involves conquest, control, and domination (as with the neurotic parent who squashes the will of his child). The stronger the leader, the more he or she is comfortable in the company of other powerful people (as with the parent who wants his children to be strong and independent).

Inappropriate control is practiced in different ways. It is found in the rigid self-control of a repressed man or woman, in the dominant and passive roles of a dysfunctional partnership, and in an authoritarian country where rulers and subjects replay the parent-child relationship. Telling lies and withholding truth are also forms of the compulsion to control situations.

The practice of exerting control over others and over life is one of the most harmful of the psychological dysfunctions. The compulsion to pursue this kind of power has its roots in the emotional memories from childhood of being at the mercy of events and the will of others.

In childhood we had no choice but to submit to the will of our parents and others. Our resistance was often futile. As adults some of us now want others to submit to us. The more we feel frustrated when our need to control is hindered, the more that our painful, unresolved feelings of inner passivity are activated. In failing to see this part in ourselves, we can become more desperate for power and control and are apt to resort to intimidation, deception, lawlessness, and militarism.

A controller, in this emotional sense, is someone who feels controlled—helpless, weak, insignificant, ineffective—when he is not doing the controlling. The McCarthy and Cold War eras were driven in part by right-wing paranoia, the irrational fear of being taken over by communism (or in the case of communists, by capitalists), just as the opposition of fundamentalists to the civil rights of homosexuals is based partly on the feeling that a homosexual agenda will be forced upon them.

William Bennett is an example of an out-of-control controller. He was dubbed the nation's high priest of morality while education secretary under Reagan and drug czar during the Bush I presidency. Bennett was exposed for his lack of self-regulation—his out-of-control gambling habit in which he reportedly lost several million dollars. A political power player who presented himself as a model of self-regulation, he denied the infantile bottleneck in his psyche and tried to impose a rigid, controlling mentality upon us all, lecturing us with moral righteousness in his books and speeches. It's so typical to dislike in others what we haven't resolved in ourself.

No one wants to be out of control. But an inner fear of that possibility raises the likelihood that control is a major issue for us. It also means that we are repressing or hiding certain feelings or facts about ourselves, including buried feelings of worthlessness and powerlessness. Control issues, meanwhile, tend to make us less capable of empathy and compassion.

This need to be in control creates an impulse to manage the lives of others. It also hides an unconscious attachment to feeling forced to submit to the will of others. When not in charge, we feel dominated and controlled. By controlling certain aspects of our lives and that of others, we create an illusion of power and independence. But all it takes is some unmanageable situation to throw us into emotional turmoil, at which times unresolved passivity rushes to the surface of our awareness as anxiety and fear.

We all have issues with control. Liberals often fear corporate and big-business abuse of power. While it is true that such abuse occurs, many of these particular liberals are anticipating an experience of passivity—intimidation, manipulation, and exploitation—which locks them into a passive-aggressive or resistant stance and makes them uncomfortable with true power. Were Big Business to stop abusing its power, many liberal psyches would go elsewhere looking for such negative, passive feelings, perhaps having to settle for acting out with a spouse or boss. Meanwhile, reform and progress are impeded as long as liberals are secretly willing to feel passive to some reactionary, controlling mentality, group, or individual. Until our psyche is debugged, we will have difficulty assuming power in an appropriate manner.

Conservatives tend to represent the aggressive energy of the controller, which is the drive of the superego, while liberals can easily identify with the passive-aggressive energy of the resister, whose inner equivalent is the subordinate or unconscious ego.

Our attachment to feeling dominated and controlled is not appealing to our self-image, so we cover it up in different ways. We can become defiant or stubborn and rebel against parental or other authority, often in ways that are self-defeating. We will defeat ourselves in order to "prove" our dislike for being controlled, when in fact being or feeling controlled is an unresolved emotional attachment that we are secretly compelled to experience.

21

How to Resolve the Daily Struggle with Control Issues

Life is not an experience that can be controlled. At best, it is to be savored and appreciated as we do our best to act graciously and make wise decisions. But a need to control is nonetheless a major problem for many of us.

This need has its source in childhood when we felt passive and had no choice but to submit to the will of others. As adults, some of us become controllers wanting others to submit, but we are frustrated by our limited capacity to impose control over events or other people. Alternatively, many of us are sensitive to feeling controlled, and we submit or react passive-aggressively, often with growing resentment and sometimes with hatred.

The issue of control has a great deal to do with our capacity for self-regulation, including the behavioral problems of addictions and compulsions as well as emotional problems such as depression and anxiety. The more we are concerned about needing to be in control, the more likely we will be out-of-control in some area of our life. The more that control issues are unresolved in our psyche, the more they rankle our social and political life.

The issue can be resolved when: (1) we recognize our tendency to experience relationships, encounters with others, or everyday situations through the feeling of being controlled; (2) we acknowledge that the feeling is caused mainly by the lingering emotional memories of passivity and submission from either the normal or the dysfunctional course of our childhood, rather than by the allegedly inappropriate actions of others; and (3) we "own" our resistance to letting go of our secret attachment to feeling controlled. (These three points are all aspects of inner passivity.)

Control issues begin to surface when a child is eighteen months to three years of age. As parents know, children resist toilet training and other attempts to turn them into civilized human beings. The child takes personal offense when his parents tell him what to do and how to do it. At the time of the "terrible two's," children scream and protest against feeling controlled. Even the gentlest parents can feel frustrated at their attempts to train their toddlers. For some children, the experience of feeling controlled is very painful. As adults we can continue to be and to feel controlled, as revealed in our struggles for self-regulation of substances and emotions and in our compulsion to control others.

It seemed to us that childhood consisted of passive experiences of giving up what we wanted and going along with someone else's will. Our childhood was filled with have-to's: *have to* go to bed, *have to* eat my vegetables, *have to* get dressed, *have to* clean my room, and *have to* be good. As adults we experience similar feelings in complying with the needs of others and performing the chores of daily life.

Many of us as children felt we had little influence on the feelings and behaviors of our parents and passively had to endure threatening or neglectful situations. We were rewarded for controlling our emotions and impulses. We were loved if we obeyed without protest. So we interpreted our obligations to our parents and to ourselves through a feeling of control. The more we felt in control, the more it seemed we could make everything work out okay.

As adults we fear being out of control, which signifies a lack of self-trust. We know, usually unconsciously, that without control we won't be able to continue to repress or hide certain feelings. Control issues cause us to clamp down on our sense of self, and they help us to keep our world "safe" by minimizing or avoiding unacceptable thoughts, feelings, or behaviors. This form of inner repression extends to others when, through the compulsion to make others act and believe as we do, we lecture them, supervise their behaviors, and determine their beliefs. This control, we feel, also makes us acceptable in the eyes of others. Otherwise, we will be seen as weak and vulnerable, which brings up buried feelings of worthlessness and powerlessness. Control issues tend to make us less capable of empathy and compassion.

However, having our sense of well-being revolve around the feeling of control creates anxiety about whether or not we are in control. In the face of life's uncertainty our control is often just an illusion. We are frequently afraid that reality will break through the illusion and that our vulnerability and helplessness before the forces of life will overwhelm us. We react and try harder to be in control and then feel even more frustrated and anxious when that doesn't help.

This need to be in charge and manage the lives of others hides an unconscious attachment to feeling forced to submit to the will of others. When not in charge, we can feel weak and vulnerable. By controlling certain aspects of our life and that of others, we create an illusion of power and independence. But all it takes is some unmanageable situation to throw us into emotional turmoil.

Control issues often sabotage romantic relationships. Consider a man with an emotional attachment to feeling controlled. In a romantic relationship his attachment produces this conflict: He will stay in the relationship because of his unconscious compulsion to continue to feel controlled, while he will want out of the relationship because feeling controlled is so painful and because it produces such negative feelings toward his partner. His inner dialogue produces words or feelings, sometimes unconscious, to the effect:

Inner critic: *What's the matter with you! How can you put up with what she demands of you?*

Inner passivity: *I hate it. I do get upset at her, and I'm going to tell her more forcefully that she has to stop.*

Inner critic: *Ha! That will be the day! She's got you where she wants you. You suck right up to her.*

Inner passivity: *That's ridiculous! I do love her, you know, despite how difficult she is. I want it to work.*

Inner critic: *I still say you like it, you passive wimp.*

Inner passivity: *No, no! Can't you see how much I'm suffering!*

Inner critic: *Well, then why don't you leave her?*

Inner passivity: *If she doesn't stop it, I'm going to leave her. I can only take so much.*

Most often, a dialogue such as this is registered only semi-consciously. Usually people experience these emotions without being aware of dialogue or back-and-forth banter. But this example of dialogue is more than just a metaphor for an emotional process. A dialogue is taking place, and we are capable of bringing the content of it to the surface. Otherwise we are at the mercy of the negative emotions and self-defeating behaviors that the conflict generates. We are establishing a foothold in the self when we witness this dialogue rather than being unconsciously entangled in it.

When we break free of the question or issue of control we find that our ego or egotism is less pronounced. Life is no longer seen or experienced through the lens of control, and we have a greater capacity for inner peace and harmony.

22

This Boss is no Democrat

The Dilbert comic-strip portrays well the horrors of having a self-serving, irrational boss. Trouble is, we all have such a boss, and our being unemployed or self-employed doesn't spare us from its wrath. This boss, the one we carry in our head, tags along everywhere and has been known to shiver our spine, agitate our stomach, and knock our knees. And it doesn't merit a personal pronoun, such as he or she. Whatever it is, it is definitely a bold and cunning *It*.

It arouses our self-doubt and questions whether we have the right to challenge authority or whether we are smart enough to be correct in holding a dissenting viewpoint. It is master of withering scorn and unequivocal righteousness. It stops us in our tracks when it asks, "On what authority can *you* say that?" If it were officiating at the polling-station on Election Day, it would glare at you, check your wrist for a democratic pulse, and, finding one, tear up your voter registration card. If you can't feel the depths of its malevolence, it has already made your blood run cold. I need hardly introduce it—we are of course revisiting inner aggression.

All along I've been saying that the mentality of the inner critic or inner aggression is the source of the behavior and attitude of the strident and ideological right-wing of political power. This energy, drive, or voice thrives in our psyche because our inner passivity allows it, and it extends its reach like an alien body-snatcher to create millions of clones among human beings, choosing in particular those with petrified egos and shallow esthetics to strut around mimicking their inner master. Dictators, tyrants, and seekers of wealth and power for their own glory are life's triumphant superegos, and they're followed around by aspiring smaller ones capable of matching infamy. Some dictators like Stalin and Mao were ostensibly leftists, but their blood-soaked authoritarianism blows their cover and reveals them as superpower superegos, psychopathic politicians whose political leanings were secondary to their lust for power.

Rulers of despotic regimes and dysfunctional democracies prefer a passive population that can easily be manipulated over a population of psychologically healthy individuals who know their value, are capable of discernment, and are prepared to overthrow incompetent leaders or vote them out of office. In despotic regimes, those who try to break out and rise to the democratic apex (which in the psyche is the self) are in danger of course of being tortured, imprisoned, or murdered. We can have a milder but comparable experience when we struggle for inner freedom. On this quest we can endure what feel like trials by fire, involving disorientation, confusion, doubt, and anxiety (some of this induced by a furious ego and superego fighting for their lives). The bravest among us, on our evolutionary leap to the other side, undergo a harrowing loss of identity and death of inner factions, until our inner leader or sovereign self is consolidated.

To stop us on this leap, inner aggression would use a shoulder-fired missile launcher if it had one. Instead it must revert to rants and rages, which escalate to hysterical denunciations of our goodness and value when we begin to acquire new insight. Insight or knowledge is power, and inner aggression is a force that shuts down on any stirrings of power other than its own. Alias the Great Manipulator of Facts, it intervenes to declare, in reference to our growing insight, *You should be ashamed that you didn't know that—it's just more evidence that you're a total loser, a hopeless fool!* It's like mocking someone because the nugget of gold he found wasn't discovered by him one day earlier. Still, this ruse often confounds us. Typically, when assaulted so, we experience shame and embarrassment. Consequently, anxiety and fear are kicked up by our resolve to change and grow, which can cause us to fall short on our forward leap.

A lot of us liberals are rebels of the passive-aggressive variety. It's as if we were saying to the right-wing, "Go ahead and rule the world, but you're not going to repress me—so there!" But being a passive-aggressive rebel is little or no threat to our superego or to dysfunctional world leaders. "Acting up" or being "bad" is usually passive-aggressive or pseudo-aggressive behavior that leads to self-defeat and produces guilt, anxiety, and shame. If on the other hand we are simply "good," we are in danger of being compulsively good, which means we depend emotionally on approval and acceptance from others, in which case we forfeit the privilege of being unique and leaving our footprint on the path of progress.

To defeat our inner aggression, we need to neutralize its malice in everyday life. In a typical example of its interference, a liberal-minded artist, who was launching a marketing program to revive his career, was plagued with self-doubt. His enthusiasm for this revival was producing an adrenaline rush, and he had plenty of energy to carry it out. But at night when he needed to rest, he couldn't turn off his mind which was churning up ideas and speculating about his prospects.

"Your relentless night-time thoughts are a reaction to your inner critic," I told him. "It's assailing you with allegations or insinuations that you're making mistakes with your marketing program, or spending too much money on it, or that you're all washed up anyway. In reaction to this negative energy coming at you, you produce through your self-doubt a host of anxious speculations, defensive thoughts, and worries about success. Some second-guessing may be difficult to avoid, but your self-doubt is like an enabler of the negative, judgmental energy that's having its way with you. If you understand this, you can start to become silent at night, as you observe the barrage of inner aggression without becoming defensive. Just see the attack as irrational, negative energy, and begin to feel that you don't have to do battle with it. You're under attack, for sure, but if you stand by yourself, understand your inner passivity, and believe in the power of your self to face down and neutralize this barrage, you will begin to experience more inner peacefulness.

"In another way of seeing it," I added, "you can't let go at night of your mental activity because you feel the success you seek won't happen if you don't push it or force it along. It feels that your mind is an expression of power, and that impression feels true to you because, in your passivity with the inner critic, you're desperate for even an illusion of power. The real power is to see your inner aggression more clearly and then refrain from being defensive and reactive with it. Soon you'll be able to neutralize it completely. Then you'll be able to drop your mental activity and find repose at night."

As we consider political strategy in moving forward our liberal agenda, we can talk about "framing the debate" in a more skilful fashion. But framing is just one aspect of the challenge. A significant degree of inner development is required on our part to demand a level playing field against the brutishness and boorishness of the strident right. Michael Moore said after the 2004 presidential election, "They beat us because they are abusers." But it might be more accurate to say they beat us because so many of us are unwitting "abusees" or ready–made doormats. That is what becomes of us when we don't know or can't feel our value. Mired still in the swampland of non-being, we cower from the boss.

23

Liberals Jump in Line for Psychotherapeutic Purge

We will have more success installing a liberal vision that guides the world if we overcome our inner passivity. Before we all rush to get in line for this psychotherapeutic purge, please stay seated for more information.

Just because inner passivity is invisible doesn't mean we can't see it. We can start with the obvious symptoms and work back to the source.

Helping in the process is our faculty of reason, God's gift to us secularists. No Patriot Act, no matter how ironic its title, can take it away. So let's be reasonable and analytical about the mystery of this so-called inner passivity. Do we really need to incorporate new knowledge about ourselves into the political fray? Consider the evidence. Feel the folly.

Quite a few of us are injustice collectors, meaning that we are unconsciously determined to experience the world as a fountainhead of unfairness cascading down upon us. Through injustice collecting, we live in either a sour, defeated way or a bellicose, complaining manner. We feel too guilty or undeserving to live in a freer, more joyful way. While we claim to be supporters of reform and progress, deeper down we can be expecting failure and disappointment (precursors for cynicism and despair) from our efforts.

Take a deep breath, fellow liberals—don't let my prickly prose upset you. Every psyche has a dark side. I know I would swear off foreign cars, Starbucks doubleshots, and maybe even my passivity if that would eliminate the dark side of the conservative psyche. No more pink elephants, either, while our yellow donkey is hobbled.

To repeat, we can also be personally and politically codependent, meaning we are enablers of the downtrodden and dispossessed. Our secret mantra: "Have pity on me and the people I identify with," is induced not by compassion but by the opportunity to identify with the plight of the dysfunctional or underprivileged and join them in an acid bath of worthlessness. Through them we soak up feelings of abandonment, deprivation, unworthiness, and hopelessness because such negativity is unresolved in us.

Can you now see the inner passivity oozing from our quivering brows? It's not a pretty sight, but once it's exposed we can wipe it away. Let's look for more of it.

Some liberals come alive and feel their best when they are in opposition to people on the right. We feel power in opposing the powerful and righteousness in identifying with the weak. We know who we are through our passive-aggressiveness. Our flag of defiance, dissent, and resistance snaps in the air. We jump to attention at a chance to be reactive to right-wing initiatives and expressions of power. But limp is our banner of authority, nobility, initiative, and self-regulation.

We practice paralyzing procrastination, often with devotion to the process. This common experience of inner passivity, when painful and self-defeating, is a product of our unconscious willingness to feel helpless and overwhelmed. It is an acting out of inner weakness and through it we fail (or unconsciously decline) to access our inner strength and represent our best interests. Procrastination also induces attacks from the inner critic—*How can you allow yourself to keep putting off that important work!*—that deepen our experience of passivity and heighten our inner fear.

Inner passivity, in the sense in which it can be said to have an agenda or goal, is determined both to be experienced and to survive. One liberal client, who had a passive relationship with his mother, sought out a similar relationship with another older woman soon after his mother died. Another liberal client complained, frequently and chronically, about never having enough time; in fact he had lots of time and only complained in order to express and accentuate his sense of being overwhelmed and therefore inwardly passive. A friend experienced winter cold as a form of torture—she was secretly willing to feel overcome by and helpless to this external circumstance she couldn't control. Another's panic attacks while driving a car had the same source: She felt like a child trying to do something beyond her ability. People who feel rushed much of the time are under the influence of inner passivity—the feeling of being acted upon by some agenda, schedule, or obligation.

Shopping for clothes, another liberal friend became upset at an aggressive saleslady who hovered at her shoulder. My friend left the store in a huff and told me a half-hour later she was still upset about it. I said, "Through your inner passivity, you were unduly influenced by the saleslady's presence. Emotionally, you made her presence a big deal, and then you covered up your role in it by getting upset at her."

"I got it! Don't say another word!"

I'm fortunate to have friends—and readers too—who tolerate my analytic volunteerism.

And bless my liberal and conservative clients who come back for more. One of them always wanted to know the why, why of things, even to tough, existential questions without answer. Her passive mother had subscribed to the formula, "If only I knew the rules, I'd be okay." One time my client became distraught because she couldn't figure out *why* a dog she had seen running by the road *was running so fast.* Anxious about it, she mulled over a dozen possibilities, to no avail. When we obsess over such questions in a way that is distressing, we deepen a sense of futility. We are framing life's experiences in such a way as to accentuate our helplessness.

Some psychologists advocate being in the "here-and-now" as a means to inner connection, but a satisfactory here-and-now state cannot be maintained when our unresolved passivity (and inner negativity in all its forms) juggles our moods and agitates our desires. We are thrown into mental or emotional turmoil, and the here-and-now experience is either not available to us with any consistency or, being available, it is rife with suffering.

One new client told me, "We have everything we need to be happy inside of us, and all we have to do is live in the here-and-now."

"What you don't have inside of you," I replied, "is the knowledge of how your aggression and passivity are entrenched in your psyche and the price you pay for that."

Inner passivity loves to be experienced. It is now quivering and bowing ecstatically before the authoritarian dunderheads in control of our government. Free of inner passivity we discover our self which bows only to the mystery, the wonder, the divine, and the well-being of the people.

24

The Need to be Right

Some of us—political extremists and religious fundamentalists—are downright uptight about the need to be right. Yet even in mundane matters, as when a husband and wife are arguing heatedly whether they spent six days or seven in Boca Raton on their wedding anniversary twenty years ago, the need to be right energizes the fight.

Sometimes more is at stake, as in who's right and who's wrong about global warming. However, whether the subject concerns climate disruption or the length of a week in Florida, the same psychological dynamics can be at play in the need to be right.

While it appears that the righteous, argumentative, or dogmatic individual is passionately concerned about truth, he is interested in something much more personal. And that is the inner comfort and emotional reassurance that he feels by allegedly being in the know, ahead of the pack, and on the side of right.

This individual is fighting not for the truth but for the glory of his wisdom, the protection of his self-image, and even for his right to exist. He'll fight to the death to protect his illusions, and for this reason irrationality, contradiction, and incivility abound.

Several emotional factors are present in our psyche when our proclamations of "truth" become too strident:

1. We depend on our ego in order to stabilize our self-image and reaffirm our self-deception. Our ego loves to be right in order to secure more validation, but ego is only one member of the family, and making it the host of our inner house is like teenage Tommy controlling the family budget.

2. When we disagree, we proceed on the premise that one of us is right and the other wrong. If I am wrong, you might be right. If you are right, then I might have to submit to your version of reality. Having to submit feels awful. It's better to resist you, even if you are right. Otherwise, you'll shove your agenda down my throat and force me, as I watch you gloat, to swallow your reality.

3. Our inner critic loves it when we're wrong. It sees a change to attack: *You fool, why didn't you know that!? Will you ever get it right? Once again everyone sees how dumb you are!* We try to protect ourselves from an attack such as this, and being right or being convinced that we're right is one of our defenses to accommodate the inner boss.

4. Being right means having the power. That's how our inner critic operates. Because it's "right," we submit to it. Therefore, if I am "right," others will submit to me. This is how I can circumvent my inner passivity, by embracing an illusion of power.

5. Next and maybe worst is our attempt to protect ourselves from the dreaded nothingness. Rigid belief gives us standing and substance in the universe. It is a foundation on which we can proclaim, "I am right: therefore I exist!" It helps us to gain weight, the leaden weight of righteousness that prevents us from floating away and disappearing into the emotional void of insignificance.

6. Last, being right allows us to exult in our distinctive superiority. The more I am right, the more I stand separate from and superior to those who are wrong. I'm right about creationism and intelligent design, which means I'm made in God's image, and thus separate from nature and better than the rest of earth-bound creation.

An evolved person doesn't fear being wrong. Who he is, his very essence, feels right. This right feeling has nothing to do with facts or even knowledge. It is based on what he feels to be the truth about his own intrinsic value and existence. His life, he suspects, is neither more nor less than the value of anyone else's. And if he's wrong about that, so what! When he's wrong, it's still alright.

25

The Dialectic of Futility (Part I)

I remember reading Friedrich Engels in college and hating that word, *dialectic.* What the #&*#&, I sputtered, does dialectic materialism mean anyway? As best I could surmise, it was about the resolution of the conflict between the values of materialism and idealism. This conflict, represented by two competing human views, went back and forth from one side (thesis) to the other (antithesis) until we sorted out the kinks in our mental processing and arrived at synthesis, a higher level of understanding.

From the time of our pre-history, we have been putting our heads together in a thousand different positions—as materialists, idealists, doers, and thinkers—sometimes comically, tragically, and cooperatively, often antagonistically knocking skulls as we have tried to survive, prosper, and figure out the meaning of life. We have become smarter through this evolutionary process, though not necessarily wiser.

Dialectics also exist between rich and poor, secularists and religious, leftists and rightists, and hawks and doves. Another important dialectic has been invisible and is not widely known. This one, which I call *the dialectic of futility,* is a struggle for authority and standing between two emotional parts of ourself—inner passivity and inner aggression. This inner dialectic is a political as well as a psychological struggle. Two opposing forces of the psyche are vying for power as they attempt to negotiate and lead according to their own bias and configuration. We humans navigate poorly in the fog of our psyche, and in this heavy mist we find ourselves drawn to one inner pole or the other, seeing the world and relating to it from the perspective of inner passivity (left pole) or from inner aggression (right pole).[11]

Here is an example of the dialectic of futility in action, one among what may be an infinite number of variations:

> Inner aggression: *You made a fool of yourself at the office today. How could you have asked such a stupid question at the meeting?*
>
> Inner passivity: *It wasn't that bad. It was a mistake to ask that question, but everybody's probably forgotten about it by now.* (Note inner passivity's defensiveness. Our inner passivity devotes much energy to reasoning futilely with irrational inner aggression.)
>
> Inner aggression: *I disagree. They're probably still snickering about it. It only proves to them that you're incompetent.*
>
> Inner passivity: *Many of them have told me how important I am to the organization. This was just a little slip-up, and nobody's perfect.*
>
> Inner aggression: *Well, that's certainly true of you. Hopelessly imperfect! With no improvement in sight!*
>
> Inner passivity: *I do try to do my best. If only I'd gotten more support from my parents.*

And on it goes, like a couple bickering endlessly. It can help to picture these voices as pop-up windows on our commuter monitor. To be effective on an inner level, we patiently "close" them—or at least gently try to close them—not attached emotionally to whether they continue to pop up or not. As mentioned, the dialectic of futility is an inner processing of our negativity, and the components of the dialectic—inner passivity and inner aggression—are conflicting negative poles to which we are emotionally tethered.

While we tend to represent ourselves and see the world from one pole or the other, we often represent one pole in one context and the other pole in another. A person, for instance, might be passive with a boss and dominant with a spouse.

When an individual is in the process of transcending the dialectic of futility, inner aggression can still invade his or her inner space. But a shift of power is occurring. Our inner sovereignty, felt through the self, is now starting to represent us in the place of inner passivity. Now the dialogue might proceed in this fashion:

> Inner aggression: *You made a fool of yourself at the office today. How could you have asked such a stupid question at the meeting?*
>
> Self: *Did I just hear some inner criticism?*
>
> Inner aggression: *Yes, you did! Do I have to repeat myself!*
>
> Self: *Who invited you in? What's this nonsense you're babbling?*

Inner aggression: *Don't think you can brush me aside so easily.*

Self: *You're silly. Go away.*

Inner aggression: *No, I won't.*

Self: *Okay. Stay around. I don't care.*

Inner aggression: *Did you hear what I said?*

Self: *I heard you. But I can't take it seriously.*

Inner aggression: *Well, you'd better. I know what I'm talking about.*

Self: Silence.

Inner aggression: Silence.

This individual is not intimidated. His attitude to inner aggression is dismissive. He doesn't take the accusation seriously and he exhibits no defensiveness. Nor does he feel any resonance with the negative charge. It's like dropping the rope in a tug of war or displaying a martial-art maneuver that throws the foe off balance. One client called the process "inner jujitsu." (Dialogues also occur between the self and inner passivity.)

A Jesuit priest once said, "The greatest trick of the devil is to persuade us that he does not exist." The same can be said both of inner aggression and inner passivity. We might only be aware of their presence by our self-doubt, anxiety, inner defensiveness, fear, depression, and so on. Our inner aggression is pleased enough to have us live in the delusion—through our ego—that we are the master of our personality, while our inner passivity hides like a phantom in subterranean obscurity.

To expose and become free of the dialectic, *we each must address the conflict in the everyday personal struggles in which it appears.* The following example shows the nature of the conflict in an instance of overeating or the eating of an unhealthy food, and how the dialectic leads ultimately to self-sabotage:

> Inner aggression: *Why did you just eat that chocolate sundae?*
>
> Inner passivity: *It was so good. But I know I shouldn't have eaten it.*
>
> Inner aggression: *Obviously it was good. But you promised to stay on your diet.*
>
> Inner passivity: *I know. I was weak.*
>
> Inner aggression: *Weak! It's worse than that. You're a hopeless slob!*
>
> Inner passivity: *I went two days without eating anything sweet. That shows I can be strong.*
>
> Inner aggression: *Who are you kidding! You didn't think twice about gobbling it down.*
>
> Inner passivity: *I know I'm going to do better in the future.*
>
> Inner aggression: *What a laugh! Do you really think it's going to get any easier in the future?*
>
> Inner passivity: (capitulating) *It's true. I'm hopeless. I do it every time. It's never going to get better.*
>
> Inner aggression: (backing off) *Look, just keep trying. You've got to stop being such a failure.*
>
> Inner passivity: *I don't know if I can. Damn, I might as well just go and eat another one.*

As in this example, our inner aggression often lightens once the individual, through his inner passivity, pleads guilty to some "crime" such as being a failure or being incompetent, or once he feels sufficient shame, anxiety, or guilt. The problem is that the individual, in allowing such a concession to be made, is going to suffer the consequences of making this concession. He is going to be convinced, for instance, that he is indeed a failure, and he will feel the consequent anguish of guilt, anxiety, or shame. Or he will give up and capitulate completely to out-of-control behavior, leading to more emotional and physical distress. Even following a concession to failure, such as the collapse of one's self-regulation, the abuse of inner aggression can start up again, possibly within minutes or hours, and the torture of scorn and derision can feel even more unbearable.

From the perspective of either the left pole or the right we are at a disadvantage in exercising wise authority, discerning truth, and finding happiness. It is the self that represents our best interests. As the self consolidates and grows, it becomes the domicile of our sovereignty. In the political context, the sovereign citizen may be politically opinionated but he doesn't lose his identity or composure in petty politics. He identifies foremost with the values of truth, justice, and service because those values, he is discovering, are principal elements of his own self.

26

The Use and Abuse of Negative Power

Negative energy and positive energy are polarities of nature. These opposing forces permeate the fabric of life, like life and death and night and day. To live in happiness and peace, we have to be clever enough to recognize the dark or negative side and protect ourselves in our unavoidable encounters with it.

The task is made more difficult when powerful people make it their business to promote and underwrite human negativity. As mentioned, our negativity is being exploited by financial interests who promote anger, dissension, and hatred through the nation's airwaves for the purpose of making money. Listeners and viewers of right-wing radio and television are attracted to the harsh, ridiculing, and condemning tone and content of these broadcasts. These individuals are thereby suckered in to committing the psychological mechanism of projection, whereby their own unresolved negativity is attributed to others. Those doing the projection and displacement become convinced that the negativity they now feel toward, say, liberals is validated by the "bad" that they "see" in them, unaware that they are seeing only what they have projected of their own negativity. This negativity feels to them like power, such that the more they hate the more they can feel they are undermining or obliterating the targets of their hatred. But this power is an illusion because, of course, it does not obliterate those on the receiving end and often instead empowers them. It does though, in an emotional way, weaken those who are doing the projecting since they suffer the full negative charge of their animosity. Projection as a psychological mechanism became part of human knowledge early in the 1900s, but ignorance of it is still astonishingly and tragically endemic.

Political negativity has been manufactured, literally, since rich conservative foundations began to pour millions of dollars into "a propaganda mill" beginning in the 1970's. In the words of *Harper's Magazine* editor Lewis H. Lapham, this message machine "has been grinding out the news that all government is bad, and that the word 'public' in all its uses and declensions (public service, citizenship, public health, community, public park, commonwealth, public school, etc.), connotes inefficiency and waste."[12]

Lapham says these re-education programs, "undertaken by a cadre of ultraconservative and self-mythologizing millionaires bent on rescuing the country from the hideous grasp of Satanic liberalism,"[13] have disbursed $3 billion over a thirty-year period to finance reactionary think-tanks, writers, printing presses, academics, publications, newsletters, and smear campaigns against liberals. A liberal activist described this siege of words as "perhaps the most potent, independent institutionalized apparatus ever assembled in a democracy to promote one belief system."[14] One of the most generous of these contributors was Richard Mellon Scaife and his foundations. In the

1990s Scaife invested many millions of dollars into journalistic and propaganda campaigns to discredit if not destroy Bill Clinton. Author Eric Alterman writes in *What Liberal Media? The Truth about Bias and the News,* that Scaife, who inherited his riches, spent many years as a mean drunk without any visible career or profession and nearly drank himself to death, time and again.[15]

Some people who are ensnared in negativity become obsessive about political power. Their negativity can take the form of an unconscious conviction that their value or substance is non-existent without having power or recognition. But the power which they do hold or acquire becomes a negative power, a way to feel superior, to subjugate opponents and reward loyalists, and to be capable of retaliation. Someone or some group must suffer, or else they don't feel the power.

In *At the End of An Age,* historian John Luckacs writes that the fundamental source of Hitler's strength was hatred.[16] Hitler's aggression and hatred fused with the passivity of the German people to create a diabolical hybrid. Such aggression and passivity lurk in the unconscious mind of all humanity. Unconscious people, acting like automatons, can fall into evil when unchecked by the dicta and wisdom of religion, law, and civilization, as well as by the knowledge of psychology, humanities, and history, or by the awareness of the self and non-duality.

We can spit our malignance out at others through disrespect, hatred, and violence, or we take it into ourselves, in escalating intensity and suffering, through forms of inner capitulation such as self-doubt, self-criticism, self-rejection, self-condemnation, and self-hatred. Intimidation and fear block us from feeling our integrity and championing our truth. Deep down, beneath civilized propriety, little has changed since the Nazi scourge because we still have not looked at our own negativity with sufficient understanding and enough will to overcome it. We do not sufficiently appreciate "evil's genius for subterranean persistence and surprises," writes columnist and author Lance Morrow in *Evil: An Investigation.*[17] Even in our everyday life we have experienced how some little "bad" thing can take over our thoughts and emotions to crowd out everything that is good.

For reasons that are complex, human conflict intensifies at certain times, as is happening on the American and world stage at the turn of this millennium. Hegel's famous dialectic of history contended that our forward progress is an ongoing dynamic of conflict and resolution. In Hegel's view, conflict leads to harmony or synthesis before moving into a higher level of recurring antithetical conflict, until that too is resolved in a positive manner. The process requires wise people who are aligned with the forward progress of society and are determined to avoid stalemate.

The struggle between the positive and the negative, good and evil, are the main themes in the recent mythologies of *Star Wars* and *The Lord of the Rings*, films that captured the popular imagination. We resonate in seeing these films with what we know intuitively: We all battle in our own way against the dark forces of negativity, even in the struggle to be cheerful as we get out of bed to face the day. In *Star Wars: Episode II—Attack of the Clones*, Obi-Wan Kenobi says, "You're focusing on the negative, Anakin. Be mindful of your thoughts." The negative, however, consumes Anakin Skywalker, and he goes on to become, of course, the evil Darth Vader.

The casting out of devils, the "carriers" of this darkness, was practiced in the Gospels, as it is practiced nowadays in the secular mode by in-depth psychotherapists. The goal is not just the eradication of evil or even the attainment of happiness but the development of greater wisdom and maturity. For those so inclined, a more evolved spirituality is also acquired. With inner negativity exposed and routed, we develop a growing rapture in the wonder and mystery of our existence—"the rapture of being alive," as Joseph Campbell put it—until our ego dissolves into nothingness and can no longer constrain our love.

The Darth Vaders of the world need to know that they are in danger of becoming nothing, of dissolving back into non-being, for polluting this world with their vile cravings.

27

The Essence of Terrorism

In our search for an understanding of terrorism and the 9/11 attack we have been busy studying political, religious, economic, and cultural factors. However terrorism can also be understood through psychology.

Terrorists of all stripes are steeped in a victim mentality. They believe they are being violated and oppressed by Western power and culture. They experience the dynamics of the West through feelings of deprivation, helplessness, domination, and defeat. Their unconscious interest is not in reform or progress but in the ongoing experience of themselves as victims of alleged injustice and oppression.

Their violent reactions, designed to blame others for their negative feelings, cover up or defend against their unconscious determination to maintain, and even indulge in, their sense of victimization and their raging negativity. By striking out with violence the terrorist can claim in his inner defense that he is not experiencing his situation through unresolved negativity. He believes that his retaliation (or fantasies of retaliation, in the case of would-be terrorists) represents power and strength.

The terrorist experiences the power of others, whether nations or individuals, through feelings of being humiliated, overlooked, and pushed aside. It is through reactive anger and hatred that he knows himself and feels his "power." However he wants to believe, as an inner cover-up or denial of the dark elements in his psyche, that his hateful impressions of others are an objective guide to truth and action.

The Islamic extremist also hates to see others enjoying freedom, and thus like all fundamentalists he is obsessed with regulating personal behaviors. He is so repressed in himself and so reactive to his inner negativity that he is compelled to believe through projection that the animosity he feels toward the freedom of others is proof that their freedom is associated with iniquity or with what is forbidden. His psychological profile includes other symptoms:

* The terrorist is enmeshed in helplessness, alienation, and despair. Suicide is an option because in his entanglement in the shadow elements of his psyche he is not connected to his essence, his ultimate value. The terrorist creates his life to mirror his inner darkness. He may feel he has little to live for other than suicidal revenge, which when acted upon represents the ultimate price for his inner passivity.
* As a fanatic his mind and emotions have been taken over by dogma or by the agenda of others, and he doesn't think for himself. He is a bewildered soul, separated from his own truth and his own self. In his search for orientation, this individual embraces a cause that makes him feel real or powerful, while

his dogma is a twisted rationalization for his inner discord.

* The terrorist feels pushed aside and rendered invisible. His pathological anti-social behavior covers up his attachment to such feelings, and it says, in effect: "I have power! I can destroy you! Now you will pay attention to me!" He is very sensitive to feeling disrespected. Yet the terrorist has little respect for the sanctity of others and no respect even for his own life.

* The terrorist's hatred is another symptom of knowing himself through hopelessness and inner passivity. Like the person who goes around inwardly beating up on himself, the terrorist is utterly passive to his own inner aggression. The greater his passivity, the more extreme is his hatred, first of self, then projected onto others and external circumstances. The greater his hatred, the more likely he will act on it. His terrorism is a defense against his seeing, feeling, and owning his own sense of worthlessness and self-loathing.

* His claim to be fighting for reform or legitimate goals is a rationalization, a cover for the aggressive and hateful impulses that spring from his inner embrace of negative convictions. If reform were truly the aim of the Islamic terrorist, he would use discourse and the power of persuasion to advance justice and democracy. His extreme negativity creates an inner desperation and a lack of patience that block this option.

* The terrorist's severe egotism accounts for his self-righteousness. He is under the influence of infantile egotism and acts from the same impulse as a child who slaps another child who touches his toy. The

terrorist feels entitled to act on his primitive emotions, particularly when he becomes bonded with a cadre of similarly emotionally impaired individuals.

Political commentators agree that Islamic radicals are united by a sense of shared alienation. Such alienation has many dimensions—cultural, political, geographical, linguistic, educational, and psychological. Many middle-class, professional Westerners also feel alienated, from themselves and in their own societies and cities. This problem stems, at its root, from the unresolved emotional issues that create self-doubt, self-rejection, self-abandonment, and self-hatred, which are emphatically psychological.

Western psychology has been ignored in the Islamic world, and even in the West a majority of us do not understand many of its basic principles. It will help when all of us can see ourselves more objectively, more profoundly, so that humanity can grow beyond primitive emotionalism.

In the meantime, we can be using psychological knowledge as well as military strength to defeat the terrorists. There must be many would-be terrorists who can be pulled back from the chasm of violence through exposure to the highest principles of Western psychology. We can speed the process by becoming examples of the benefits of that knowledge.

28

The Emotional Virus behind Hatred and Youth Violence

High-school shootings and other forms of hatred and violence are due in part to self-hatred, a psychological condition that has been difficult for authorities to understand and accept. The teenage gunman Jeff Weise, who shot and killed classmates and then himself in Red Lake, MN, in early 2005, revealed his emotional problem with hatred and self-hatred in his interest in and explorations of Nazi websites.

From childhood all of us absorb some of our natural aggression, and this aggression is directed back at ourselves as inner aggression. In milder forms, it is experienced as self-criticism. In its more self-defeating forms, as mentioned, it intensifies to self-negation, self-condemnation, self-rejection, or self-hatred.

A hateful person isn't likely to be aware of the antagonistic relationship he has with himself. He convinces himself that somehow his targets are deserving of his hatred. But he is projecting his self-rejection and self-hatred on to others. To cover up his own self-hatred, he hates others for allegedly rejecting and hating him, or he hates them because he "sees" their hatred of him, which is his projected hatred reflected back to him. Or indeed, his projection of his hatred causes others to reject and hate him in return.

In the case of high-school shootings, students who have personality disorders can have a particularly difficult time regulating or moderating their negative reactions to feelings of being rejected or bullied by others. The negativity they feel coming at them from others fuels their own self-hatred, causing a more intense projection of that hatred outward to others.

Negativity runs high in young people with personality disorders or borderline personality disorders. A psychologist may need several hours of talk and testing with a child or adult to determine whether such a disorder exists. The behaviors of people afflicted with such disorders cannot be predicted with any certainty. Improved teaching of psychology in our schools would greatly help young people to manage their lives. Both emotionally stable and unstable students can benefit from a better understanding of psychology. Teachers need a good understanding of these deep dynamics in order to pass the knowledge along to their students. Now when psychology classes are taught, the course material is simplistic and homogenized and does not penetrate into the emotional plight or reality of students trying desperately to come into harmony with themselves and others.

Our children need to be taught that bullying and hatred are reflections of one's own relationship with oneself. In hating others, a person is revealing the hatred or rejection he feels for himself. If a student begins to look inward with this understanding, he is in a position to recognize the ways in which he doesn't like himself, to understand that this dislike is irrational and emotional, based on unresolved emotional attachments and on his identification with a limited and painful sense of who he is. With the right knowledge he can start to break free from this condition.

In this process, we see the fallacy of blaming others for our emotional reactions. Or more precisely, we develop the capacity to understand the source of our negative impressions by seeing the conflicts and attachments of our own psyche. At this point, we are less likely to act out antagonistically or violently toward others.

Cliques are a fact of life in the nation's schools. Students use the clique's acceptance and validation to override their inner doubt and conflict. The left-out losers get to feel more intensely their non-acceptance, their self-rejection, and their perceived insignificance and worthlessness. The same dynamics are at work in students who become members of gangs or students who succumb to peer pressure to begin smoking.

Confusion arises over the best teaching methodologies because many mental-health professionals, in not having penetrated their own inner depths, discount the influence of subconscious forces and describe violence as learned behavior from parental, social, and cultural influences. But how do we account for the fact that many abused children become respected citizens? Or that respected citizens and good parents can produce anti-social children? A violent society or violent parents can certainly have a negative influence on young people—but where does this violence originate? Its source is the negative energy and conflict that inhabit every human psyche.

When we are brave enough to face ourselves, we see our capacity for evil and violence in our human nature. As an example of our instinct to deny this, Luke Skywalker, in fright and disavowal, attacked the evil image of himself that he saw reflected as Darth Vader in the cave where Yoda sent him. Unless we take responsibility for this hidden darkness in ourselves, we remain in denial, susceptible to its covert and dangerous impulses.

The dark side of our nature was previously kept more in check by influences such as religion, kinship, and a slower pace of life. Modern influences such as the availability and lethal power of firearms are thrusting upon us an immediate need for greater self-understanding.

29

The Dialectic of Futility (Part II)

From the right side of the dialectic, our inner landscape is a military system with its sniping, surveillance, and assaults. From the left side it is a diplomatic system of negotiation, compromise, and stalemate. The result is a form of inner corruption that compromises our role as citizens.

When caught in the dialectic, we often can't tell the difference between positive and negative strength. The negative power of the inner critic can feel like something normal or natural, a voice that, though negative, is nonetheless part of the inner "family" of voices. We can believe as well that the forceful, defensive reactions we express through inner passivity are also positive, such as when we react indignantly to someone's request for a favor because we interpreted the request as a form of disrespect or control. Even passive-aggressive behaviors, such as ignoring an obligation or a request, can feel like strength, although they are ultimately very passive and self-defeating. Or we believe that reactive anger, which is often a cover-up for our inner passivity, is a positive force.

The dialectic erodes and corrupts our power. It's not just power that corrupts but also the lack of power. Corruption is not simply a factor of the misuse of power, as leftists say, but is also linked to a *lack* of power (inner passivity).

Elements of this corruption can be seen in domestic abuse cases. The victim of a wife-beater contributes to the acting out of violence through her inner passivity. A strong woman free of passivity would not be involved with such a man. The passive victim, however, has not achieved the inner development through which she holds enough self-esteem to know emotionally and absolutely that such treatment of her is totally unacceptable.

Ironically, the abuser is also passive. Although it appears that his problem is violence and anger, he is feeling passive somewhere in his life, perhaps in his dealings with his job, boss, customers, or clients. If he is unemployed or in a low-paying job, he can feel stuck, blocked, trapped, and hopeless. He often feels out of control with drugs, alcohol, or emotional problems. To compensate for his own inner passivity, he can be desperate to feel some form of power. He is then compelled to become cruel or abusive to someone he perceives as more passive and helpless than himself, namely his spouse and children. For him, even destructive, abusive power feels better than his passivity. This so-called power also serves to cover up his emotional indulgence in that passivity. The problem is further complicated by the severe inner reproach that both the abuser and the abused direct toward themselves.

To take a political example of the corruption caused by passivity, the politician who pockets money in exchange for favoritism would seem to have an undue desire for the feeling of power or the accumulation of money. Where does that desire come from? Something is missing in this person's own sense of self. This person, limited in his personal development, is corruptible because he has not accessed inner richness, the fulfilling sense of power and integrity that come from knowing himself more completely. His corruption is founded on a lack of power, a disconnect from self that is a principle symptom of inner passivity. For him, integrity and service are secondary to power and money because he is desperate for some external evidence of his value.

Neither polarity in the dialectic of futility will be dormant for long. And when one becomes activated, the other follows, triggering the dialectic process. Our creative potential is dissipated in this inner conflict between these two conditions—inner passivity with its sense of helplessness, anxiety, and disconnection, and inner aggression with its negative carping and unabashed authoritarianism. We become more disengaged as citizens as this impasse intensifies, and for each of us mired in this condition our democracy becomes increasingly dysfunctional.

This inner conflict strongly influences our sense of who we are. Our experience of this dialectic becomes our thoughts, emotions, beliefs, and actions. Some people know themselves much of the time through the experience of their inner passivity, some through their inner aggression, and most of us much of the time through our experience of the clash of these two negative conditions. (Psychoanalysis speaks of the tension between the strict superego and the subordinate ego, out of which emerges the painful emotions of guilt and shame. Much has been written in psychoanalytic literature about the superego or inner aggression, but less is written about inner passivity.)

The more we react to inner aggression, the stronger it gets. Reacting to it intensifies the dialectic impasse. We have to simply observe it, understand it, expose its irrationality, and feel our determination to become free of it. Often we don't need words or dialogue to neutralize this inner aggression. Once we have identified it, silent observation of it along with a feeling of self-support and self-respect can be enough to stare it down. More and more this feeling becomes a belief in self and a connection to self, which is the basis of inner strength and true power.

Our inner aggression is relatively easy to expose, though it can be difficult to neutralize. In contrast, however, our inner passivity is more difficult to identify and overcome. It is a deeper, more subtle configuration in our psyche. Most of my clients can agree they have a nasty inner critic, but they struggle to bring inner passivity into focus.

Often, as an unconscious defense against exposing inner passivity, we plead guilty to being "bad" or deficient in some way—i.e. being lazy, a failure, an angry person, or a dull personality—rather than acknowledge the deeper problem (our inner passivity). We cling to our defenses (such as being lazy or a failure) and suffer self-defeat rather than own up to our inner passivity. We then carry around a painful, limited sense of self, which contributes to depression as well as personality and creativity impairments regarding work, relationships, and social and political involvement.

To repeat this vital point, the essential feature of self-defeat or self-sabotage: *For the defense to work and to cover up inner passivity, the person must be willing to believe he is flawed in some way and, as the price demanded by the inner critic for this alleged shortcoming, to accept disagreeable feelings about himself, leading to emotional difficulties and lowered expectations.*

Often the defensive gestures we make when entangled in the dialectic of futility can feel to us like an appropriate expression of strength. While on a diet one might say, for example, with the emphasis on I: "*I* am choosing to eat this dessert," or, when trying to control alcohol consumption, "*I* am going to stop after this next drink." In these examples, we are actually being passive, though trying to save face with a pretense of control and power.

An observation from science presents a model of the dialectic in a biological light: A young woman had her corpus callosum, the tissue that connects the two hemispheres of the brain, severed by surgeons because she was suffering from extremely debilitating epilepsy. An article from *The Scientific American Book of the Brain* describes the results:

> Although the operation alleviated her seizures, she was left with two centers of consciousness vying for dominance. When asked if her left hand feels numb, she shouts, "Yes! Wait! No! Yes! No, no! Wait, yes!" her face contorted as each of her two minds, only one of which can feel the hand, tries to answer. The researcher then hands her a sheet of paper with the words "yes" and "no" written on it and tells her to point to the correct answer. The woman stares at the

sheet for a moment. Then her left forefinger stabs at "yes" and her right forefinger at "no."[18]

When we expose the dialectic, we are seeing how much our inner passivity allows our inner aggression to hold us accountable and lord it over us. We are in thrall to the guerilla operations of the dialectic dynamic. The autocratic force of inner aggression second-guesses our choices and decisions, and, as mentioned, punishes us with disapproval and reproach for the smallest misdemeanors. But our inner passivity makes us willing (albeit unconscious) participants in the process. At the dialectic level, the militarism of inner aggression is excessive, while the diplomacy of inner passivity is inept. Hence, we are contaminated by an internal corruption that facilitates corruption on the national scene.

30

Inner Aggression's Role in the Abortion Debate

The abortion option presents women and men with an opportunity to flounder in self-doubt. We ask ourselves, "Do I have the authority to terminate the life of this fetus?" Our inner aggression objects to our attempts to assert such authority. It is especially able to attack and condemn us for a decision that is morally ambiguous and to which large numbers of people fiercely object.

The veto power of inner aggression reveals itself in other ways, for instance, when we agonize over whether to pull the life-support system on a dying loved one or whether to euthanize an old or sick pet. A woman whose inner passivity is substantial can be tortured by her inner critic for years after having an abortion. For a man, a comparable anguish is possible for agreeing to the procedure. They may turn to religious authority in order to be granted a sense of forgiveness. The guilt and shame produced by the inner rebuke is proportional to the extent of their inner passivity.

The abortion issue is wide-ranging, of course, and the role of inner aggression is just one aspect of it. Still, many anti-abortionists are unaware of inner aggression and how it shapes their point of view. They believe they know all that is relevant about the abortion question, yet their position is emotionally biased and abetted by a lack of self-knowledge. The pro-choice lobby needs to expose our inner authoritarianism and show how it has made the abortion question so confounding.

Those who oppose the abortion option as well as personal choice in matters such as medical marijuana and euthanasia are often determined to see these issues in moral rather than psychological terms. Ardent anti-abortionists are compelled to placate their inner aggression and cover up their fear of it, so they cloak the issues in moral language. In other words, their righteousness comes down on the side of inner aggression and thereby spares them from its wrath. They experience that aggression indirectly, however, through their condemnation of the pro-choice community (the negative energy has to be expended either outwardly or inwardly).

Their assumption that abortion is morally indefensible corresponds with their inner experience: They can feel the prospect of inner condemnation in making or even in contemplating such a choice. Our inner aggression, however, cares nothing about right or wrong but only about control, domination, and the continuance of its illegitimate authority. Nonetheless, it will frame the issue in terms of morality when our self-doubt includes moral ambiguity, which then effectively throws us under its influence.

Passivity to the inner critic, or fear of it, creates a deep resentment toward those who are freer in their beliefs and actions. People are not pleased to see others feeling free in a way they cannot. They compensate by feeling morally superior, believing whole-heartedly, sometimes with righteous fervor, in this cover-up of their own unresolved negative emotions. When the inner critic calls the shots, however, people sacrifice their intellectual integrity and confer moral authority upon their inner aggression as well as upon external claimants (pastors, politicians) to such authority.

People can also become convinced that abortion is wrong because, unconsciously, they identify with the helplessness of the fetus or with the fetus being unwanted and unloved. This tendency to frame the issue in terms of helplessness and rejection is due to conflicts or attachments that are unresolved in them. They deny this or cover it up by generating anger at those who, allegedly, do not respect the value of the fetus. So an anti-abortion stance can also be based on inner passivity as well as inner aggression.

It is important that we evolve toward greater personal authority. It is the framework of our sovereignty and our democracy depends on us having it. The person who expresses her personal authority looks for orientation, direction, and strength from within herself. Though not always free from self-doubt or bouts of negativity, this individual believes in her value, and is able to express this sense of value calmly and resolutely, expecting justice, respect, and non-violence in dealings with others. This person does not make the mistake of "trying" to be positive. Such contrived posturing is compulsive goodness, which is a person's need to try to be good because she feels so guilty, shamed, or worthless when not being good or when not "performing" at a high "moral" standard. Instead, when this person's inner conflict has been quelled, she is natural, gracious, and perceptive.

This sovereign individual listens to others and considers their perspectives, but she doesn't look to them to identify her place in the universe or to define her role and weigh her essence. She can confront ideologues and authoritarians because she has neutralized her aggressive inner critic. She may be more interested in understanding who they are rather than in being upset at how they oppose her or differ from her.

In terms of the abortion issue, she is able to consider all options and all beliefs and then make a decision based on belief in herself and trust in her wisdom.

Being our own wise authority confers a great sense of freedom. We are not going to be children doing what we are told. We want to discover the range of wise inner authority and make that the law of our personal domain. We want to incorporate civil rights and the Bill of Rights into our sense of self. What could be more obvious and noble?

Here at the cusp of history, in a slow and arduous struggle for the evolvement, if not the continuation, of our species, we are heroes leading the way against the darkness of our own ignorance and fear. Of course, much progress has been made and we have been advancing the spirit of the Enlightenment. The work goes on, requiring now that we attain the personal authority to be comfortable with choices that once we undermined from within.

31

Our Psyche is Ready for New Software

I'm always in danger of losing readers when I begin to write about our emotional attachments to negative feelings. Hence, I've inserted this chapter toward the back of the book. I also try especially hard to make this topic lively and interesting, though on this subject I feel like a stand-up comic making fun of disabled children.

Yes, that's how our psyche takes in the topic of emotional attachments, with a groan of disgust. This X-rated knowledge is banned by our inner censors. Observe yourself as you read along and see if your brain doesn't start tripping over vowels, begging for sleep, yearning to clean the stove, or inciting you to hurl this book against the wall.

What does that mean, to be *emotionally attached*? I have been sprinkling the term in the text to this point, and now I elaborate. To our great detriment we indulge in negative emotions. We secretly look for and embellish on feelings of being deprived, refused, controlled, helpless, criticized, rejected, and so on. We are reluctant to give up our attachment to these negative emotions despite the suffering and self-sabotage they bring about. Our unconscious negativity consists not only of the negativity itself but also our secret readiness to experience it and to hold on to it. This is the dirty, dark secret about ourselves we are not supposed to know.[19]

This knowledge is vital to our struggle to make America more democratic. When we hold on to our negativity, we hold on to our passivity and aggression as well. We have a conflict of interest: Consciously, we want to be powerful and free individuals, but in our psyche resides this dark, secret interest in continuing to experience ourselves in the old way, through unresolved negative emotions that have haunted us since childhood and the human psyche for millennia. Consequently, we don't feel freedom and sovereignty deeply enough. This old inner software can constitute, in a significant way, our (emotional) identity. We don't know who we are without all this negativity.

To break free is also to know ourselves in a revolutionary new way. Who will we be without our complaints, anger, and defeats? Can liberals, with all our inner passivity, be the vanguard of a progressive democracy in fact instead of fancy? Isn't it hopeless with all those reactionary forces lined up against us? Can we be powerful, aggressive, and even ruthless when necessary—and compassionate too? Up to now, it appears, we haven't been able to secure our progressive vision because it involves the creation of a new paradigm for ourselves, not just for society. *If we don't see how reactionary we are internally, and how determined we are to hold on to the old paradigm of negative attachments and associations, how can we possibly create a new world order of peace, harmony, and greater freedom?*

Often when I tell people about this inner state of affairs, they say something like, "Well yes, that makes sense; I have no quarrel with that; I think that does describe our problem." But as soon as their own personal negativity is exposed and addressed in the context of their emotional attachment to it, they are full of denials, defenses, and deflections. If the reader reflects for a moment on this contention that we are emotionally attached to our negativity, he or she may feel some hesitation or unwillingness to go deeper into a consideration of that possibility. The reader will likely find it difficult to penetrate into the meaning of this claim in any way that seems helpful or illuminating. We feel that to accept this claim as true implies we are fools or simpletons for being so blind or obtuse. How could we be dim-witted enough to want to hold onto our negativity, when obviously it only creates suffering and self-defeat? Did I say this knowledge is humbling and defies common sense?

Some readers might say that we are physically addicted to a biochemical mix that creates negative emotions. But what produces that particular mix? We can go in circles asking what came first, our negativity or the biochemical mix. Brain research is looking for an understanding of our emotions in biology, but we would be unwise to wait for scientific studies of the brain to solve the problem of human negativity. In *Looking for Spinoza: Joy, Sorrow, and the Feeling Brain,* Antonio Damasio writes, "The fact that we, sentient and sophisticated creatures, call certain feelings positive and others negative is directly related to the fluidity or strain of the life process." In other words, he writes, positive and negative experiences "are determined by life regulation."[20] Surely our great human drama—the historic, evolutionary struggle between the positive and the negative, good and evil—is more than a problem of physiological impediments.

In *A User's Guide to the Brain*, Harvard psychiatrist John Ratey doesn't mention the psyche at all (unlike the brain, the psyche, the seat of consciousness, can't be put under a microscope). Ratey does write about "the essence of consciousness," which he says is "the feeling we have of owning our actions and being able to develop our self-conceptions through experience over time."[21] I would amend that definition to say "to develop our self-conceptions through experience, *knowledge, and practice* over time." His thesis, like that of neuroscientists in general, contends that vital new intelligence to facilitate this process will come from brain research. I say *yes, maybe*—though I am skeptical. While scientific materialism certainly saves lives with new medicines and procedures, can it produce a higher knowledge or wisdom, as the understanding of our psyche can, that transcends the material realm, revealing to us, one at a time, the greatest truths, for instance, on the meaning and purpose of life—more specifically, on the meaning of *your* life and *mine*?

In contrast to the view of these brain researchers, I perceive that the struggle to clear away what is unhealthy and negative in ourselves is a heroic undertaking that gives each of us a chance to be a noble, sovereign being, not just an animal or a biological system at the mercy of fluidity. In the meantime, for the *immediate* purposes of personal and world peace, our psyche can tell us so much of what we need to know.

By penetrating our psyche we can clear away whatever blocks our happiness and the vision of our destiny. We see before us the good and the bad. The good is our shining self, an inestimable inner treasure through which we can feel a deep, profound sense of the unique being that each one of us is. The bad is the inner or deep negative, the shadow or enemy within, that weakens us like a virulent mold in the rafters of our attic—the invisible, toxic air we unknowingly breathe. We destroy mold when we take it out of the dark and expose it to light. The negative—the inner mold—cannot live in the illumination of our awareness.

When we are negative, we are really not free. We are not free of fear, or hate, anger, loneliness, envy, greed, and passivity. Freedom from such negativity also makes us more intelligent—we are no longer coddled, deceived, or manipulated by illusions, denial, distractions, tricks of the mind, and various defenses. We no longer whine and complain to cover up our readiness to resonate with negative experiences. Now we can feel our sovereignty, our legitimacy, and our inalienable right to respect and justice.

32

Freeing Ourselves from Negative Feelings

The question I am most frequently asked by my clients is, "How does this process work, and how can I free myself from negative thoughts and feelings?" We have to gain insight into the way we feel and how we perceive reality. Certain principles must be accepted emotionally and worked through. Specific steps can be followed.

1) We recognize that we won't change how we feel about ourselves and others by focusing on external conditions. We might be able to produce a temporary high or escape from negative feelings by running away, changing locations, acquiring a new lover, making more money, and so on. But a permanent feeling of well-being is dependent on a breakthrough into a deeper awareness of the roots of our emotional reactions.

2) Rather than repress our negative perceptions and emotions, or express them inappropriately, we must discover the origins of our propensity to interpret the actions and behaviors of others as somehow against us. We start by creating an inventory of

childhood feelings and reactions toward our parents and siblings.

3) Next we establish an inventory of our current feelings about our relationships, career, and self. Then we compare these feelings to those we experienced in childhood with our parents and siblings. We look in particular for emotional patterns that repeat themselves throughout our lives. Insight occurs when we see how we carry over any unpleasant childhood perceptions or misperceptions into the present. We are compelled to repeat what is unresolved in our psyche no matter how repressed those emotional memories are or how painful the repetition is.

For instance, a person who as a child felt overlooked and undervalued will unconsciously look for opportunities to experience those old feelings in his adult life. This person sees others getting more attention or validation than he does, and he is hurt and feels devalued. But this person is unconsciously willing to interpret the actions of others as against him because that emotional attachment is unresolved in his psyche. Whatever is unresolved in us is determined to be experienced repeatedly. Usually we can't change the behavior of others; we can only change our willingness to use that behavior to feel unloved and unimportant, or to feel other unresolved emotions such as deprivation, control, helplessness, rejection, and criticism.

4) We see that we interpret our life and relationships through the child part of our psyche. Children are naturally self-centered. They believe they have the power to cause others to feel a certain way. They feel

> that everyone's eyes are focused on them. They see the world as "for them" or "against them," and are focused on what they believe they are entitled to. We can be very slow to relinquish this self-centered perspective when we grow up.

Insight and understanding create an improvement in how we feel about ourselves, others, and our lives. When we see objectively, we free ourselves to make clearer, centered decisions about what to do. Old ways of suffering and negative reproaches wither away, leaving in their place new feelings of confidence, contentment, and serenity.

For many people, the compulsion to experience the negativity in their psyche is so powerful that success in escaping this condition can be their greatest lifetime achievement. We have to want very much to live in a freer state of being. When people see clearly the configuration of their entrapment in negativity, they are greatly empowered and motivated to become free.

Anger and greed are also symptoms of this negativity. As stated, a person's anger toward others or external circumstances is very often a cover-up of, or a defense against, his unconscious willingness to indulge in emotions such as deprival, helplessness, criticism, rejection, abandonment, and other passive experiences. His anger convinces him that his suffering is due to the insensitivity of others or the unfairness of life. But this is how he deceives himself. His anger towards others or towards circumstances is his way of convincing himself that others are to blame and that he is not secretly indulging in some variation of his own negativity. For instance, he can be angry at people who are apparently rejecting him, though the source of his problem is likely his emotional attachment to feeling rejected as well as his self-rejection.

Consider a person who chronically feels unloved. Deep in this person's psyche, he or she "snuggles up" to old familiar feelings of being rejected, abandoned, or criticized. This person ends up with spouses, lovers, or friends who are limited in their capacity to love. The consequence for this person is to feel unloved and perhaps unlovable. Whether in fact this person is loved or not is often irrelevant in the sense that, either way, he or she secretly seeks out the unresolved self-rejection. Just a look of indifference from an acquaintance or an old memory of being jilted can trigger it.

Now it is easy for such a person to drift into related feelings of being neglected, overlooked, disrespected, not wanted, and unloved. He has a hard time loving others, and tends to overlook, disrespect, criticize, and reject them, just as he feels is done to him. He unconsciously creates or stumbles into situations, both in reality and in his mind, where he is entangled in these feelings. At idle moments or when, say, sitting at his desk at work, he produces imaginary scenes which constitute his indulgence in these negative feelings. Memories of shame and regret pop into his mind. He bristles with anger from slights felt long ago. He also encounters such negative feelings in his dreams. Becoming depressed is the common outcome. Depression, a side-effect of our negativity, produces political indifference and weakens our democracy.

If such a person's parents were unloving toward him and each other, then he is more likely to have this attachment. But it doesn't do any good to blame parents. Doing so deepens a sense of victimization. Blaming parents is also a defense that allows us to avoid taking responsibility for our attachment in the present moment to feeling rejected (or to any of the other negative attachments).

When we see our negativity as emotional attachments, we understand that we can free ourselves from it. We have to understand *the power and determination of this part of ourselves to be experienced.* Whatever is unresolved emotionally is going to be experienced over and over. We have a compulsion to act out what is unresolved, and unconsciously we will even go looking for opportunities to suffer in this manner. The negative has a life of its own, and it certainly will not cooperate in being reduced or exterminated.

Sometimes we can pare the negative issue down to the bones, meaning to a few sentences or paragraph of content, which we can then assimilate as an essential truth about our psyche. The content has to be accurate and apply directly to our issue. I composed this message for a client and gave it to him to read every day until he soaked it in past his resistance. The "I" in this statement applies to him, of course:

> I keep hearing, "I should be happy, I should be in a relationship, I should control my feelings, I shouldn't complain, I shouldn't be wasting time or wasting my life." That voice or feeling or implication that *I shouldn't* is the voice of my inner critic. It is irrational and negative. It has no business passing judgment on my life. I now see that I have been passive to that voice and defensive with it, and have allowed it to hold me accountable. I am watching that voice more closely, and I am declining to answer it in any defensive way. I

> am starting to take it much less seriously, as it has no rational standing or legitimacy. I can feel that I am connecting to myself and am less entangled in inner passivity or self-doubt as I watch for that critical, aggressive voice or feeling and am able to neutralize it by not giving it credence and thereby not reacting to it.

As we get rid of our negativity, we begin to feel the significance and the value of the unique person each of us is. It feels as if freedom is our middle name. Now we know intuitively—as long as you or I or the next person feels this way—we cannot be defeated by reactionary elements. We can say to the enemies of freedom, knowing it is true: "I will not surrender my freedoms. They are inside of me. I could not give them away even if I tried. Nor can they be taken from me by dictate, decree, or detention. I feel they will never be extinguished." As reactionaries experience us, they will feel they are up against a power they don't understand and can't suppress. They will be routed by an invisible force until, at some point, many of them are absorbed into the new paradigm.

This state of evolvement is not a utopian dream. It is earthy and gutsy because attaining it requires a courageous encounter with our psyche and the deep, unconscious negativity we harbor within. I have released a large chunk of this negativity in myself, and undoubtedly have more to disburden. The benefits are now obvious to me. I wouldn't take back an ounce of that negativity for a million or a billion bucks.

33

THE THRILL OF NEGATIVE PEEPING

Practitioners of the psychological "vice" of negative peeping abound across the political spectrum, among rich and poor, and throughout the world. This "vice" is driven by unconscious negativity, and it offers us ways to experience both inner passivity and inner aggression.

Negative peeping is the act of looking for some sight, object, or impression for the unconscious purpose of experiencing an unresolved negative emotion. Negative peeping is more than just seeing the glass half-empty: *It is our inner determination to find half-empty glasses to look at and, when inevitably we find them, hence to feel deprived, refused, controlled, criticized, or rejected. It also consists of looking for opportunities to project our unconscious negativity onto others.*

Negative peeping is an unconscious compulsion that is practiced universally. Seeing and understanding it, and then catching ourselves in the act of doing it, opens up a treasure chest of self-knowledge. Of course, we want to deny that we peep in this way—*I look at what I want to, not what some inner program dictates.* Whether we are looking at beauty or ugliness, our eyes are likely to be directed by emotional factors.

Why would a person be drawn visually to something that brings up a painful feeling when hundreds of other more pleasing sights or objects can be observed? He or she is fulfilling unconscious negativity's yearning to be experienced. Negative peepers almost universally don't know how willing and ready they are to stir up those feelings and absorb them in a way that creates a variety of consequences, such as feeling anxious, depressed, lonely, resentful, angry, or worthless.

There are thousands of examples of how against our best interests we commit this "crime" of negative peeping. A Jewish friend sent me a greeting card that, she said whimsically, referred to the Jewish version of negative peeping: "One's own poverty doesn't hurt as much as someone else's wealth." This refers, of course, to the painful feeling of envy, a form of suffering produced by an emotional attachment to feeling deprived or refused, which can be facilitated by negative peeping. Often the more that the item we crave is out of reach, the deeper the pain of envy. Envy is often experienced through peeping, and someone determined to suffer in this way will find in rich America much at which to peep. Conservatives often accuse liberals of opposing wealth disparity out of envy—but they won't legitimately be able to make this accusation once we refrain from negative peeping.

What are other important reasons, in the political context, for understanding negative peeping? This peeping is a significant way our negativity is acted out, and negativity in all its forms weakens our resolve and dissipates our energy. The more negative we are, the less we care about the higher values our nation is commissioned to represent. We might be able to appreciate our nation's glorious past, but we can't see and hold a vision for its future progress. We usually can't create what we can't visualize or imagine. Through negative peeping, the future we see is likely to be more of the injustice and oppression we decry, and which, regretfully, we remain emotionally aligned with continuing to experience.

To work it out, we need to see how this activity intrudes into our everyday life. In one version, people who are always going into the kitchen to poke their heads into the refrigerator think they are looking for what is good to eat. Secretly, they are looking to see what's *not* there. Why? To absorb the empty feeling of being deprived or the feeling they are missing out on something. Someone looking out the window of their house could be engaged in negative peeping if, say, this person felt a jolt of enmity toward a neighbor or felt trapped indoors because it was a rainy day. Another common experience of peeping involves fixating on the apparent happiness of doting couples who are observed, say, walking in the mall or on the street. The secret purpose of such peeping is to feel alone, abandoned, and unloved.

When, as in the last example, we indulge in such inner passivity, we quickly become a target of our inner critic: *How come you have no one in your life, you loser!* Or, *You might as well give up now on ever finding love.*

A person is also peeping when, standing in front of another person, he is not seeing that person for who that person is or might be, but rather he is seeing a reflection of himself through the eyes of that person. In other words, he is seeing how he thinks the other person is seeing him, which corresponds with how he secretly wants to experience the other person's impression of him. He might see a good reflection of himself, in which he is all decked out in a confident persona. Or he might see an unattractive reflection, as if he is coated in a Cinderella ash of lowly unworthiness. Either way it is negative peeping because he is not seeing the other person objectively but instead is using the other person either to defend against his attachment to feeling criticized or rejected *(he admires me)* or to experience directly his attachment *(he disrespects me).* This form of peeping is much more widespread than we might imagine.

Our peeping can be very subtle. Comparing ourselves unfavorably to others is a common variation of it. On the surface we want to feel good about ourselves, but in our unconscious depths the story is different: Here we snuggle up to feeling that we have little value. The media and their visual images now provide devout couch-potatoes a thousand chances a day to compare themselves unfavorably to others, especially celebrities, in a subtle inner process that goes undetected. Only in the last one hundred years or so, since mass circulation magazines appeared, have we had these images of so-called superior people thrust in our faces every day. I believe this is one of the big emotional challenges young people face. It doesn't help when they are exposed to commercials that proclaim, "Be like Mike (Jordan)." I say to young people, "You are unique. Be true to yourself. Happiness comes in feeling your own value." To meet this challenge of living in a silly culture, where celebrities are promoted as paragons of superiority and the products they hawk as trademarks of quality, we have to value ourselves more deeply, no matter how invisible we may be to the culture or the media.

Our consumer society gives us many opportunities to peep. A person can think he is innocently flipping through a glossy magazine when, deep inside himself, he is experiencing twinges of regret in feeling deprived of the advertised seductions. A driving force behind consumerism is the need, as a defense, to disprove our attachment to deprivation, refusal, or the feeling of missing out on something by going out and buying it. We are then driven to use the feeling of "getting" (merchandise) to cover up our participation in the painful sense that something vital is missing from our lives (connection to self). Often we go deeply into debt (self-sabotage) in maintaining this defense.

Readers with a peeping inclination can easily detect this mechanism in themselves if they are alert and watchful. Be more conscious of where your eyes go and what you find yourself looking at. Did you consciously make a choice to take in this or that impression? Correlate what you are looking at with what you are feeling or thinking. Assess that feeling. Is it negative or positive? If you can slip past your defenses, you can expose unconscious negativity. It may seem ugly, but don't be fooled: A gram of self-knowledge is worth a ton of diamonds. We are now in a position to free ourselves of our emotional attachments to unresolved negativity.

We can also peep into the past or the future, using our memory or imagination in ways that cause suffering, which is the subject of the next chapter. We frequently remember events or situations that produced pain or grief, and we recreate vivid visualizations through which we replay the event. Sometimes it is hard to stop remembering something that was very painful. Time can heal such wounds, but we can unconsciously keep these wounds open and prolong our suffering through negative peeping and by misusing our imagination.

34

Misuse of the Emotional Imagination

Liberals are capable of imaging scenarios in which the right wing, holding political power, creates more anti-democratic laws, institutions, and systems, until finally we have been stripped of power and citizenship. In passivity, we create our version of paranoia in which we dwell on the prospect of such a future and, in some cases, indulge through our imagination in the helplessness and agony of it happening. (This is similar to negative peeping, but is conducted through our imagination instead of directly through our eyes.)

The more we do this, the more such danger exists. We become, in self-sabotage, secret wishful-thinkers (or cocreators of such eventuality) through our indulgence in such a possibility. The stronger we are, the less we dwell on such an outcome as we live our lives in the myriad of healthy ways that block tyranny and promote democracy.

When we talk about a liberal vision, we had better include the emotional blockage of that vision. In psychoanalysis, the emotional imagination is called *the visual drive*, which is understood to mean the creative life force, the symbolic expression of our humanity that includes our emotional association with images, metaphors, pictures, ideas, and concepts. Yet, even while this symbolic life surfaces in creative expression, the roots of this life force are unconscious. Writers of literary fiction often claim that their ideas, characters, and plotting originate through a conscious mental process, and they are reluctant to acknowledge that much of their work is an unconscious sublimation of unsettled issues in their psyche. In other words their work is transcendence through art of issues they are not necessarily dealing with consciously. The unconscious ". . . remains, in the healthiest and best adapted of human beings, a repository of powerful irrational forces," writes Peter Gay, a biographer of Freud.[22]

The emotional imagination can be used either for our pleasure and benefit or for our displeasure and harm. When we are not conscious enough, our emotional imagination is usurped by the negativity in our psyche and used for dark or at least self-defeating purposes—our indulgence in the negative. This is further complicated by the advertising imagery and metaphors of our culture that invade our psyche—hyped commercial messages implanted in our mind by ceaseless repetition—that can pollute the myths, images, and symbolism that can give meaning to our life. We can see the power that visual imagery in the form of television and video games has over adults and children, and how passive we can be in coming under its spell. We take for granted the powerful effect of these moving images, forgetting, for those of us who experienced television's origins, how enthralled and truly mesmerized we were when these images first invaded our homes more than a half century ago.

Worriers especially are flagrant abusers of the imagination. Their creative capacity is being misused in a way that generates anxiety. When that happens, we begin to focus on painful memories from the past, or we embellish upon unpleasant circumstances in the present, or we make dire speculations and considerations about the future. When our imagination is entangled in such a way with our emotions, we call it the *emotional imagination.*

Through the emotional imagination we conjure up visions of worst-case scenarios. We convince ourselves that it is somehow important to think about or to visualize all the bad things that could happen any day now. However the worrying person in creating his grim tomorrows is cultivating the feeling of being helpless, deprived, and abandoned *right now*—in the here-and-now. Of course, many of the things about which we worry—painfully, sometimes fearfully so—*never happen!* That doesn't matter to our unconscious negative agenda. Because of our secret willingness to collude in our unresolved negativity, we don't need facts or reality to generate negative impressions and consequent suffering.

Often the root of worry is our compulsion to experience the feeling of helplessness. A person, for instance, who worries about his children being injured or killed, or about his house being burglarized or his stock portfolio crashing, can perhaps take a few precautionary measures. But ultimately, we have limited control over future events. The fact of our limited control becomes entangled in our inner passivity to produce anxiety, worry, and fear. (In past centuries, superstition and fear of evil forces were earlier forms of inner passivity's influence over our imagination.)

Another insidious misuse of imagination involves what one client termed his "skeet-shoot." Despite having a college degree and intellectual interests, he had been working as a waiter for several years. He regularly came up with plausible ideas for more satisfying and creative work, but within a short time he had managed in his mind to shoot down these ideas and quickly lose any enthusiasm for them. The process of undermining himself involved, through imagery and speculation, his wholesale production of possible problems and obstacles in his career path that he felt would be insurmountable. This "skeet-shooting," which left him miserable and dejected, served his unconscious readiness to go on living with himself through a familiar, painful paradigm, that of being an underachieving individual who simply did not have the power to carve out his destiny. Again, this clash of his inner passivity and his inner aggression (which assailed him for being a hopeless dead duck) left him shattered on the grounds of his shooting range. It felt that he had no more control over his life than the outcome of a movie he was watching.

To stop misusing our imagination, we have to become more conscious and inwardly alert. We have to clear our vision of negative scenarios in order to fulfill ourselves and create a great democracy. We must establish a positive vision in our imagination before it can be actualized.

35

Enthusiasm for Injustice Collecting Stalls Progress

Liberals and conservatives are equally adept at injustice collecting. This nasty form of unconscious acting-out refers to our readiness to experience an injustice, or what we are willing to interpret emotionally as an injustice, because doing so induces an unresolved negative issue in our psyche.

The injustice collector, as mentioned earlier, reacts with indignation and protest when he observes an injustice, thereby obscuring his secret indulgence in an unresolved negative experience such as feeling deprived, helpless, discounted, or rejected. A healthy person, in comparison, may observe an injustice and decide to take steps to address it, but he doesn't secretly use the injustice to stir up unresolved feelings.

Under the influence of injustice collecting, we are not sincerely interested in remedying or reforming an injustice, or in feeling compassion for the victims of it, despite our protestations to the contrary. We do not want to give up our precious injustices: Who will we be without our suffering? We don't step into that kind of freedom overnight.

For people on the right, injustice collecting tends to be more personal, while on the left we frequently make it more about the plight of others or the inhumanity of a cruel world. More precisely, injustice collectors on the right prefer to imbibe personal victimization, with customized enemies and "unfair" circumstances that affect them directly. Liberals prefer a substitute course—identifying with the plight of others or suffering from the folly we perceive in local, national, and international situations. But like conservatives, we will certainly make do with friends-and-family incitements when a juicy opportunity arises.

Injustice collecting is often the driving force behind political activism, which is a case of us doing the right thing for the wrong reasons. Philosopher Jacob Needleman, author of *The American Soul: Rediscovering the Wisdom of the Founders*, describes in his book's preface a scene from the 1970s when he and colleagues were discussing the Vietnam War. One person was ". . . speaking of America with contempt, condemning not only its war policy but the whole structure of its government . . . America was hypocritically betraying all that it claimed to stand for. American corporations were raping nature and the world. The media were under the thumb of American greed, blanketing the earth with a global consumerism that was destroying the values of simpler, nobler cultures."[23] The speaker's negative tone prompted another person, an elder at this gathering, to say in mild admonishment, "You don't know what you have here. You simply don't know what you have." If we look deeper we understand that the young speaker's hostile criticism of America had much to do with his own negativity. In the late 1960s and early

1970s, I was like that young speaker, and I remember many times berating the U.S. government with similar hostility, while agreeing wholeheartedly with others who expressed similar contempt.

Of course, outrage can be appropriate when blunderers are wreaking havoc, but I know now how much my outrage harbored my own negativity. When we criticize or attack with this kind of emotionalism, we feel that our negativity is validated by the corruption, cruelty, or stupidity of those we are denouncing. The negativity however is within us and is based on various unresolved issues in our psyche. When we don't recognize and take responsibility for it, we remain part of the problem.

Injustice collectors might approach the poor under the pretext of being helpful, but they are often driven by guilt and the need to justify or redeem themselves from inner-critic accusations and attacks. I remember when I lived at the Catholic Worker residence in the Bowery how much the regulars at the soup-kitchen disliked condescending and guilty "do-gooders" who were often nice liberals. As a Catholic Worker in the mid-1970s, I served soup and cleaned toilets on the Bowery. There I absorbed some of the movement's liberating credo. I was infused with the power and joy of personal involvement at the very heart of life, and I was called upon to recognize the importance of each person and to embrace those who might hate me. Whether in the Bowery or the bowels of Calcutta or in front of our TV set we have to be inwardly astute to avoid an unhealthy identification with struggling humanity. Feeling compassion is healthy and feeling inspired to help others is normally appropriate, but identification with feelings of deprivation, helplessness, and a sense of failure produces a useless and painful negative experience. Often we believe we need the "energy" of distress and anxiety to inspire our reformist impulses. But it is more likely to fuel a desperation or anguish that helps no one.

Sometimes from a distance, slouching toward armchair liberalism, we project our issues of passivity and helplessness onto the masses and wonder why God or the government is not doing more for them. Usually we rationalize away any resulting misgivings or guilt about our privileged circumstances, managing also to stifle twinges of compassion so that we don't have to go downtown and look those poor souls in the face. What a shame, we say, they are not treated with more respect and value, as we meanwhile sneak into their skin and cozy up to the feeling of being disrespected and devalued, overlooked and marginalized, which are the negative emotions we can feel in our own relationships to each other and to right-wing power, and which we are loathe to acknowledge and most certainly to give up.

Representatives of the left are capable of pointing out with brilliant argument the right's inconsistencies, contradictions, and cruelties. When we are injustice collecting however, our points are apt to be made with a negative, bitter, or condescending tone. On the right the recipients of this reaction then react themselves to the negativity rather than rationally to the argument. People on the right are often struck by the left's negativity, leaving them convinced that leftists, progressives, and even liberals hate America. The claim is that "the angry left" is lost in the fog of its own ire. When the right detects negativity coming from the left, this negativity is seized upon to discredit valid perspectives. People on the right, projecting their own hostility on to us, are super-sensitive to negativity and can feel validated and triumphant in having "exposed" it somewhere outside of themselves. Stalemate ensues and irrationality deepens in a dialectic futility.

Injustice collecting can appear among scholars and intellectuals. Emotionalism can taint their scholarship, determining what information they select as pertinent and how they interpret the data. Smart people can erect more clever defenses and, in taking pride in their intelligence, can be particularly unwilling to see their self-deception. Just as negativity can hide behind the Bible or the flag, it can hide behind intellectuality, scholarship, reason, and the law.

When entangled in injustice collecting, we produce irrationality which infects the body politic. As Wendell Berry comments, "That in an age of reason, the human race, or the most wealthy and powerful parts of it, should be behaving with colossal irrationality, ought to make us wonder if reason alone can lead us to do what is right."[24]

That's right: Reason is not pure or powerful enough when the knowledge of emotional conflict and attachments is not made conscious. Common sense is not sufficient to protect us if we haven't dug up all the facts. We need to expose and assimilate the knowledge that identifies injustice collecting as unnecessary suffering and a failure of self-regulation.

36

Inner Voices Disappear with Conscious Surveillance

Back in the old days my inner voices could dislocate the armature on an audiometer. Things quieted down when I learned to sit back and watch the interplay between the two voices that disturbed me the most, those of my inner aggression and inner passivity.

Providing we don't take sides, the dialogue between these two antagonists can be quite entertaining. As a witness, we can relax with a beer or a coffee or a happy smile, observing the emotional discord with a degree of separation. Using this technique, our voices quiet down, deflated because we're no longer hanging out in the middle, pummeled like a piñata doll.

First we have to learn to recognize and identify the voices. This requires an inner watchfulness. The following example illustrates the learning process. A client was struggling with her freelance writing career and having difficulty promoting and marketing her skills. In fact, her procrastination was extreme, and for several months she had not taken steps to find writing assignments from regional and national publications. She received occasional calls for her work from editors, and she performed their assignments well. But the amount of work was insufficient for her to support herself.

She told me that each morning for months she had been waking up and saying silently to herself, *Oh God. What will I do today?* This voice of inner passivity set the tone for her day. Typically, she shuffled around all day without direction or purpose. By the end of the day her inner aggression was attacking her fiercely: *You blew the whole day! You have nothing to show for yourself! You certainly ought to be ashamed.* She did indeed feel ashamed, even as her voice of inner passivity mumbled excuses and offered defenses. Unfortunately, she was now primed to repeat the painful pattern the following day.

On mornings when she had a lot of chores on her agenda, her exclamation, again of inner passivity, was significantly different: *Oh my God! I have so much to do today. Where will I start?* As she pondered the question, feelings of being overwhelmed and helpless swept over her, along with anxiety and fear. This unconscious expectation lay behind her anxious morning exclamation: *There is no way I will be able to get anything effective or creative done today.* Deeper still was her readiness to experience herself in this helpless way.

This recurring dysfunction indicates the power of our attachment to the experience of inner passivity. As this client was working out this attachment, she had dreams in which admirable, beautiful people intervened in her life. In these dreams, she often felt deep love for these individuals and she would awaken feeling very good about herself. I told her that these individuals represented higher aspects of her self and that inner consolidation was underway. Like a flower in bloom after a long drought, she was moving through the conflict between her self-doubt and her inner critic, into the discovery of her emotional independence, her personal authority, and her self.

Our self is very beautiful and very powerful, and our inner aggression is no match for it. Through the discovery of our self, the old authority vested in our inner aggression begins to dissolve, while inner passivity also melts away.

Body language, as well as inner voices, can reveal inner conflict. This client had a distinct body-language motion that reflected inner passivity. Whenever she considered a course of action that challenged her, she stiffened and threw up her hands, palms outward, at the level of her shoulders in a gesture of surrender. She had been doing this motion for years without considering or understanding its significance. It directly reflected inner passivity in that moment. Stopping that motion was part of the working-through process.

The following inner voices or feelings can express inner passivity: *What am I going to do next? I promise to do it tomorrow. What if I fail? Nobody appreciates or understands me. How come nothing ever works for me? What am I going to say to him?* A religious person might express a sense of helplessness or futility through the words, *If God wills it*, or *Only God knows*. If we are considering becoming, say, politically involved, that voice, fearful of the repercussions, might say, to this effect: *You can get in a lot of trouble. Let other people take the risk. One less voice is not going to matter.*

The voice of inner passivity often sounds warnings to us, insisting, for instance, that we are in danger of being betrayed, cheated, or physically harmed. This voice claims it can be trusted and that it is revealing to us a harsh but necessary truth: *That boyfriend can't be trusted* or *That friend is going to knife you in the back.* Of course, an intuitive voice does sometimes represent our best interests. But if we have too much self-doubt in our psyche we don't know what voice to trust.

Inner passivity often comes across as a worldly voice of experience that claims to have our best interests at heart. Like the voice of the inner critic, it presents itself in the guise of an expert. "It feels like a core voice," one client said, "and that's why I give so much credence when I hear it." The more we surrender autonomy to that voice, however, the more we are left feeling frightened, vulnerable, and overwhelmed.

While inner aggression easily usurps the role of conscience, the voice of inner passivity is likely to be our tempter: *Oh, go ahead and have another drink;* or, *It won't hurt to stay in bed and miss work today;* or, *Do it, she'll never have to know that you were unfaithful.*

Sometimes inner aggression and inner passivity use the same words, so the tone or harshness of those words becomes a clue to the source. Consider the statement, *You never do anything right.* If heard or felt as an accusation, then inner aggression is speaking. If heard or felt in a softer tone with a sense of futility or self-pity, then inner passivity is talking. It's important to know the difference because precision about inner dynamics speeds up the clearing-out process.

37

Resolving a Personal Issue Benefits National Unity

It is encouraging to know that the issues we need to resolve for our personal happiness are also very important for national progress and unity. Put another way, we can ask ourselves, "How do my unresolved emotional issues contribute to our national discord?" We all have pockets of emotional conflict in our psyche, so this is a question all of us can ask and address.

Consider for example, fear of abandonment, a common emotional issue. Many of us have felt abandoned at times by friends and loved ones. Fear of abandonment is often felt acutely by an adult who as a child experienced emotional abandonment, the death of a parent, the threat of abandonment, the separation of parents, or the physical abandonment by a parent. This fear makes it more difficult for us to embrace our responsibility as citizen-watchdogs of government, for in this predicament is buried a level of self-abandonment and self-devaluation. And with self-abandonment comes the possible abandonment of everything else that we would be expected to hold dear, including our nation's integrity and ideals. With this issue, we are compelled to abandon what is precious to us.

With this issue, as well, we aren't likely to have a vision for ourselves or a sense of higher purpose, just as we don't have a vision for the country or believe strongly in, or even relate to, its ideals. We won't be able to pass along an abiding belief in the self to our children, which means we aren't bequeathing to them a convincing enough feeling of our freedom and value. Often the best we do is to identify with the power or the glossy image of our country and its power-brokers, thus to become a pawn at the disposal of others or a pseudo-patriot who uses his country and others to support his flagging sense of self.

How can we be effective citizens, as well as good parents, when this unresolved issue of abandonment creates self-absorption and makes our pain our first priority? Our vision of an American nation that embodies virtue is clouded, and just as we can't access our own virtue we have a harder time identifying virtue among the candidates for political office.

Many of us felt at least somewhat abandoned in our childhood. Even when parents were present, our feeling of abandonment developed from an implicit family understanding: *Who I am and what I think, or what I have to say is of little value.* Because we are so subjective as children, we can sometimes feel this way even when our parents are doing their best to be kind and considerate. Obviously this negative impression or emotional conviction can deeply influence our sense of self. Though we feel the pain of this negative impression we are not usually conscious of it as an emotional overlay nor are we able to articulate it as a source of our suffering. Later in life we don't appreciate how strongly it dilutes our sense of ourselves as citizens, and we are not able to feel, for instance, that *we* are the proprietors of this nation and that government officials are *our* employees.

What do we need to know to work out an issue such as fear of abandonment? Our fear indicates an unresolved attachment to the feeling of abandonment, which means on a deep inner level we expect to experience abandonment and are even compelled to replay or to create experiences of it. So this attachment carries with it the increased likelihood that abandonment in some form will indeed be acted out. We can provoke abandonment through our worry or fear, our constant need for reassurance, and our transference of our worst expectations onto another person. The other person, it is important to understand, is often tempted unconsciously to participate in this acting out and may "give" to us what is being anticipated, namely abandonment, even though doing so is painful and self-defeating for all concerned.

Fear of being abandoned represents one price we pay in suffering for this attachment, but it also serves as an unconscious defense that goes like this: *I'm not looking for that old unresolved feeling of abandonment—can't you see how much I worry or fear that it could happen (or is happening)!*

Again, though paradoxical, this fear is an indication that we are very much attached to the feeling (and even the prospect) of abandonment. The more fearful we are, the stronger the attachment, and the more we are likely to imagine an experience of abandonment or secretly be awaiting a chance to act one out.

We keep experiencing abandonment—and, emotionally and unconsciously, *wishing* to experience it—even when consciously we very much want to deepen our relationship to a loved one and live happily with that person. We transfer this expectation of abandonment to the people in our lives—to a spouse, partner, friend, or children—and live through the fear that we are being (or soon will be) abandoned.

Indications that an attachment to the feeling of abandonment is a significant problem for a particular person include chronic loneliness, helplessness, homesickness, convictions of being undeserving and bad, feelings of neglect, and acute distress on hearing about lost pets or children.

The inner dynamic described here in relation to abandonment also applies to many other negative, emotional attachments, including feelings of deprivation, refusal, helplessness, criticism, and rejection. All of these attachments operate secretly within us, and they have now been caught in the act of disrupting our individual lives and the harmony of the commons.

38

Democracy Needs Us to Find Our Voice

The downtrodden and dispossessed of the world have struggled to find their voice. They have had great spokespeople and eloquent leaders, of course, but too few of them. It may be that the chorus of their multitude isn't heard from the mountain top because they don't feel their value deeply enough.

Perhaps no emotional pain is greater than the inability to represent ourselves effectively. And no ineptitude is a greater threat to social justice and universal freedom, since power tends to become corrupted when it encounters passivity. This is a consideration for America too, where many of us, the well-to-do included, haven't found our voices either, and where the corruption of power undermines our democracy.

Most of us can make headway at becoming better communicators of our feelings, which means being able to express our hurt and distress as well as the heartfelt truth of our goodness and value. The voice that speaks from our innermost self connects us to others in the healthiest way. The following examples present insight into the emotional predicament of individuals struggling to find their voice.

Jenny, a liberal college-graduate in her twenties, was struggling to overcome feelings of being unimportant. She would sit quietly listening to her boyfriend talk at length about football, saying to herself all the while, "Doesn't he know I'm not interested in this subject." Occasionally, she told him so: "You know I'm not interested in football." Before long however, he would again be excited about the subject and be talking to her about it.

Jenny told me there were other subjects as well that he talked passionately about, and which she felt indifferent to. When she objected, he would ask, "Well, what do you want to talk about?" At this point, she said, "my mind shuts down and I can't think effectively. Even though I often do talk a lot, this is one time when I can't think, and of course I feel foolish and inadequate."

Jenny's inability to think at such moments is a defense, as well as a consequence of her unconscious negativity. Inwardly she claims that her mental paralysis (which is concocted internally as a defense called negative exhibitionism) is her problem, for which she feels bad about herself. But the deeper issue is her willingness to sit and listen to others speak passionately on a subject, while she sits dispassionately feeling empty, as if she is nothing but a sounding-board. Her unconscious negativity is her compulsion to know herself through this painful passivity, while its consequences are her inability to represent herself more effectively along with the pain and limitation she feels for allegedly being defective.

The sense of our truth and independent points of view will not be accessible for some of us until we take action to expose and work out a deep conviction of our unworthiness. One passive client told me that he couldn't access his feelings in his dealings with his critical, controlling wife and that he didn't even know what he was feeling, except that it was very painful. I told him that he had to find positions or points of view, especially the expression of his emotional needs and self-respect, which he could represent in his dealings with her. "For instance, you can tell her that her yelling at you in the car is unacceptable," I said. "Or you can tell her that you are not going to continue helping her brother with his finances unless your effort is more appreciated."

"But that will only make her angrier or more critical," he objected sharply. "I'm not sure I can contend with that." (We can feel upset, stubborn, and angry when called upon to break out of our passivity. It feels as if too much is being asked of us.)

"If you want to grow, you have no choice," I replied. "If you're going to hold your ground with her, you must access the feelings that represent your sense of truth, integrity, and fairness. You don't have to be angry to do that. Nor will you have to be stubborn. As you connect with yourself, you become more articulate and steadfast in holding your own against her because you're supported by feelings of self-respect and self-love."

Clearly, we resolve this communication problem through our personal effort. We have to care enough about ourself, and maybe our nation too, in order to try our best. The first challenge is to acknowledge our self-doubt and our (often unconscious) resonance with feelings of worthlessness. Then we must face the inner fear that has us convinced we have no right to believe in ourselves. That's the time to reach deep inside, silently waiting for a voice that wells up to affirm our goodness. That voice will be heard and believed in if we keep coming back to the well.

39

Our Emerging Self

It appears that over the centuries the inner cosmos we call the self has been developing and consolidating. This crystallization of self can be both a secular and a spiritual achievement, and it is happening now for millions of us. Like the moon thinking it's the sun, though, we're frequently mistaking ego or personality for self. Until three or four centuries ago, the lives of ordinary people were not considered important enough to be cast as heroes or heroines in stories, myths, and dramatizations. Instead, gods, kings, queens, and lesser nobility pranced on center stage. Beginning in 16th century England and France, more people began moving upward out of the class in which they were born, acquiring an evolving sense of self and with it growing freedom.

In a review of Mechal Sobel's book, *Teach Me Dreams: The Search for Self in the Revolutionary Era*, Professor Alan Taylor writes:

> Before the eighteenth century . . . most Americans and Britons had a weak and porous sense of self, one subject to the demands of their communities and their social superiors—but especially to the tricks of

> the devil and the ultimate providence of God. The few common people who wrote surviving narratives seemed to experience life passively as one surprising crisis after another, all revealing their helplessness before the ultimate and inscrutable power of fate and the divine. . . This began to change after 1740, as most people gradually reimagined themselves as assertive actors at center stage in lives with individual patterns and profound significance.[25]

Our understanding of freedom has also been evolving over many centuries. At the time of the Puritans, writes historian Eric Foner, the concept of liberty ". . . meant submission not only to the will of God but to secular authority as well . . ." In *The Story of American Freedom*, Foner writes, "The unrestrained individual enjoying natural rights, whom later generations would imagine as the embodiment of freedom, struck these Puritan settlers as the incarnation of anarchy, the antithesis of liberty."[26] Now unfortunately, many individualists believe that freedom means *license* to do whatever we want for our own alleged benefit providing it is legal. This form of "freedom" limits our happiness and is capable of producing great suffering in an increasing disconnect from one another.

The meaning of the word *self* has always puzzled psychologists. I believe their attraction to a scientific psychology, with its superficial emphasis on behavior and mental and brain processes, was in part a face-saving retreat from the challenge of this problem. Self can't be detected in the brain or in a set of statistics. Nor can it be detected in one's personality, for personality is persona, the manner and style we present to the world. Personality can be as much of a false self as is ego. Our self is much less visible and, like democracy, it represents a higher form of government (self-government) that requires our participation in its evolvement.

On the bedrock of self, we can observe the retreat of self-doubt, self-reproach, and self-blame. We have an enhanced ability to remain calm and self-possessed in difficult situations, and we decline to take things personally and react defensively. This connection to self gives us more capacity for career satisfaction, relationship happiness, and self-regulation. We can trust in life and in the value of our perceptions and feelings.

Knowing one's self is a feeling of connection, like having a twin, soul mate, or ideal dance partner joined at the heart. When we fall in love with someone, we know the love is both real and precious, even though nothing of material substance makes itself visible, except perhaps for some particular brain, heart, or respiratory activity. Again, when we discover and then realize our self, we can't see a concrete "something" representing self. But we know we have found a great inner treasure, and we can feel that it is ours to keep.

Each person's discovery and development of his self helps to frame, consolidate, and define his purpose, his way, and his truth. Through our self we find direction and purpose that is aligned with the common good and the principles of democracy. But there are many levels of clarity on the road to this discovery. Religious or secular fundamentalists, for instance, sincerely believe they have discovered truth and that they know themselves adequately if not fully. One test, however, for having discovered self and truth is in the reduction of our negativity. This achievement enables us, in the liberal tradition, to be able to maintain our equanimity and graciousness in the face of those who proclaim opposing views. However any liberal or conservative with an overabundance of inner negativity finds it difficult to be gracious or inwardly calm in such instances. If there's only one person we hate, our negativity is alive and well and we have separated ourselves from the whole. Even what we believe is true love can't be trusted as such because our unconscious negativity limits it and also has the power to eradicate it.

Connected to our self, we are capable of detachment, which indicates an absence of negativity. Detachment does not mean that we are indifferent: It means that when engaged in a struggle for justice or the promotion of other liberal values, or even when just being in the world and observing it, we can avoid feeling negative. Our negativity "hooks" us into conflict, or we are secretly interested in identifying with another person's negative experience. Once free of our hooks, we become detached.

There are many inner experiences of peace, harmony, and connection. They include a sense of God or of gods, of a Higher Self, non-dual awareness, blissful stillness and silence, and self-remembering. In these experiences we may have no object of awareness. Awareness can hover in space—it doesn't settle on anything, and it expands rather than contracts. This state of grace is purely existential, in harmony with being alive, with existing and with being existence. We may look at something, and yet there are no words describing what we think it is. Beyond that state of awareness is consciousness without content, even of self. One such impression is our embrace of unity or non-duality. After such reverie we return with our soul well sated. "Learn to walk in the sweetness of the possession of your own soul," D.H. Lawrence wrote in a 1922 essay.

A client recalled that when he slipped into a state of inner acceptance and peacefulness one evening, enjoying a serenity that was quite unusual for him, he suddenly became restless and turned on his TV, on the pretext he might be missing something important. His experience of serenity dissipated. He had succumbed in that moment to his resistance to inner growth and connection to self. Later he said he was determined to recapture that feeling of connection and not be so easily fooled into relinquishing it.

Gloria, a liberal who was struggling to develop a stronger sense of self, was feeling assailed by her negative thoughts. "I don't like where my mind goes," she said. "It's all so negative." She had a dream in which she was in a room with a friend. She decided to leave and drive to an unspecified destination. On the drive she encountered strange, scary people walking along the dirt road. "I pretended I didn't see them," she said. "I tried to ignore them and to keep moving on past them. They looked dirty and mean, and I was afraid of them and their facial expressions as they closed in around me. I thought, 'Oh dear, I left my friend back there. How can I get back to her and warn her.' I was afraid these scary people would prevent me from turning around and going back to her."

The menacing people in Gloria's dream represented the negative elements in her psyche, as well as the negative thoughts that flooded her mind, and her friend represented her self. In the dream, she was easy prey to the negative influences once she left her friend. Connected to her friend, however, the negative was kept at bay.

As a child, Gloria had felt invisible to her parents and her siblings. At that time, "I came to the conclusion that I wasn't worth being paid attention to." She tried to get attention, she said, "by being a show-off and by making sure I had a good figure." Now, however, Gloria felt lonely and unappreciated. Where she had once felt oblivious to others, she now was oblivious to her self. She understood this lukewarm appreciation she had for herself, and she promised herself she would overcome it.

I recommended that she look for opportunities each day to check in with herself. This practice involves taking a few minutes, even a few seconds, to go inward to visit with her "friend," as the Persian poet Rumi called the self. She was to seek snatches of time throughout the day to acknowledge and to remember her self, just as she would do with a loved one or dear friend. As time passed, this relationship would grow and her self would be established as a stand-by-me friend.

Many of us feel nothing in particular when we try this procedure. However, we need to persist. We try to believe in ourself, that we can make this deeper connection to our being or to existence. Sometimes we have to wait patiently in silence for our friend to come. We can't force this to happen. We usually have to wait for our mind to quiet down, which can take several minutes or more. Focusing in the moment on our breathing helps still the mind, since we are unable to think and simultaneously concentrate on our breathing.

In this practice, we are likely to encounter recurring negative thoughts or impressions that block inner accord.

If we witness or examine these, we can acknowledge and "own" our specific attachments, which is the most important step in eliminating them.

This quest for self involves the search for value and truth at the core of our being. It is not a mental exercise because our mind can penetrate only so far into the mystery of being. This plunge into the darkness within is a mission of secular faith—a belief that you, me, and everyone is worthy of a voice and a vote in the evolving society we are creating.

40

Epilogue

Can there be anything more important to believe in than our own self? Is there a better source of true power? Instead perhaps, if so inclined, we can believe in God. But wouldn't God, like any good parent, want each of us to grow up and become a fulfilled, joyful, and powerful person? Or we can believe in the nation and the Constitution. But don't the nation and the Constitution depend on our strength and vision to uphold their values, ideals, and words? If so, we are back to ourselves. It is our job to make that happen.

We can strengthen ourselves, according to literary critic Harold Bloom, by reading and studying classical literature. Bloom, who has scolded our universities for undermining intellectuality in national life, believes the study of the best classical literature is vital to our psychological health. He writes, "Ultimately we read—as Bacon, Johnson, and Emerson agree—in order to strengthen the self, and to learn its authentic interests."[27]

I agree that the classics are important for the cultivation of a sense of self. And, indeed, the civilizing, harmonizing influence of our universities might have declined. The classics are positive influences that are teaching our young important aspects of heroism and the nature of good and evil. Nonetheless, our best immediate hope for substantial personal and national growth, I believe, lies directly in self-knowledge. However, we are not inspired to self-inquiry by the scientific psychology that dominates university curriculums and emphasizes observation, testing, statistics, and mind or cognitive resources over the illuminations of psyche.

In *Shakespeare: The Invention of the Human,* Bloom highlights lines spoken by Richard II, in the play by that name, shortly before Richard is murdered. In this soliloquy, which includes the line, "I wasted time, and now doth time waste me," Richard says:

> And straight am nothing. But whate'er I be,
> Nor I, nor any man that but man is,
> With nothing shall be pleas'd, till he be eas'd
> With being nothing.

Blooms calls the soliloquy, "the earliest Shakespearean litany of nihilism," and says that Richard's "poor self has no faith in salvation," and "his desperation can conceive of no escape."[28] I believe these four lines from the soliloquy are amazingly profound and pinpoint a vital source of power and a means to understand our common cause: *We can never be pleased with ourself until we become at ease with our nothingness.* This paradoxical human plight is just what the gods, in divine wisdom and creative mischief, would find endlessly amusing: Requiring that we humans, to discover ourselves and know and feel that we are of some essential value have to accept or even embrace, in the surrender of ego and all artificiality, that we are nothing.

It is like going through the nothingness of a black hole in space, our carcass seared of all its dross, to find on the other side our divine selves at play in a parallel universe. It is in a sense what the mythological princess, Psyche, did in becoming the handmaiden of Venus: She humbled herself, set out to do the impossible, and achieved immortality.

In Hindu lore, tales are told of the *Nothingness*, the subtle, invisible essence that pervades the universe. In one tale, a son asks his father to teach him the meaning of reality. The father tells his son to look inside the seed of the great *nyagrodha* tree. The son looks and sees that there is nothing inside the seed. From this Nothingness, says the father, the mighty *nyagrodha* tree has come into being. "Thou art that, my dear son. And this is the reality."[29]

Embracing Nothingness makes us all sublimely equal and precariously vulnerable. No one is better than you or me. According to this knowledge, our essence is not matter but energy that can be either formed or formless. As we know from quantum physics, the study of matter at microscopic levels, matter seems to consist only of emptiness or nothingness. The tiniest traces of matter (if it can be called matter) may have no mass and be only energy in motion. This corresponds with the understanding of theosophists, those searchers in the realms of metaphysics, who say that matter is a secondary, not a primary, form. Matter is supported by a great formless consciousness behind it all, this view contends, and observed reality is the interplay of consciousness, energy, and matter. Consciousness is everywhere we see space, time, and form. Without the attention and presence of this enlightened consciousness, matter would scatter into chaos.[30] The opening words of the *Tao Te Ching*, a text almost 3,000 years old, allude to this mystery: *The Tao that can be expressed/ Is not the Tao of the Absolute./ The name that can be named/ Is not the name of the Absolute.*

Scientists studying subatomic activities say their presence as witnesses to such an experiment influences the dynamics of what they wish to study. Quantum mechanics shows us what we pretty well already know: Events are influenced by our presence even when we are simply onlookers. Is not a child's play on the soccer field affected because father or mother is watching on the sidelines? On the political playing field, a passive population standing on the sidelines is actively contributing to authoritarian trends. Such passivity obliterates various checks and balances, and it creates a vacuum that unhealthy personality types rush to fill. Conversely, an engaged, knowledgeable population creates a government that reflects a more evolved citizenry, while the deeper knowledge that inspires personal development propagates wiser political leaders.

In my cosmology, space, time, energy, matter, and consciousness come together to form, for each of us, our unique constellation, a motional alignment or configuration that represents our being, yet is also a continuum with the All. When we discover this self, we connect with something that, though diffuse, invisible, and formless, is very real to us. It is as formless as mercy, compassion, or love. Yet we trust it, we believe in it, we know it. We are no longer children afraid of the dark. If we are not afraid of Nothingness, we are afraid of nothing. Through the self we hold the center, whether in Nothingness, in the chaos of earth's negativity and irrationality, or up against the harshest right-wing vehemence.

Now it is easier to accept our vulnerability and understand what that means: We must grow and become wiser and more peaceful. However, we have rushed to clutch at something concrete whenever we have begun to feel vulnerable. "Indeed, at the core of superpower syndrome," writes Robert Jay Lifton, "lies a powerful fear of vulnerability."[31] We have given ourselves a nuclear arsenal to manage this fear. But in the paradoxical way of psychological reckoning, that which we fear the most is what we are most in danger of acting out or bringing down upon ourselves. Sure enough, instead of protecting us our nuclear arsenal and globally disseminated nuclear technology make us more vulnerable, in the same way that using wealth for security makes us more fearful and insecure.

It appears that the ancients, the peoples of the first world, knew more about the All than we do. We could all die out if we don't listen to the voices of "those original human cultures that lived in naked and reverent intimacy with nature . . . ," writes Andrew Harvey. He continues:

> What do those voices have to tell us? They tell us of our essential 'inter-being' with nature; they tell us of the mystery of the world we inhabit, which they know to be everywhere sustained and saturated with divine presence; they tell us of the necessity of profound respect for everything that lives and happens; they tell us of a peace that is the birthright of all those who honor the Great Web of Life; they tell us of the urgency of humility before the majesty of the universe; they tell us again and again of the depths of our responsibility as human beings to be guardians of the natural world.[32]

We can study these cultures, and read their stories, prose, and poetry, such as this passage from a Chinook blessing litany:

> We call upon the forests, the great trees reaching strongly to
> the sky with earth in
> their roots and the heavens in their branches,
> the fir and the pine and the cedar,
> and we ask them to
> Teach us, and show us the Way.[33]

Some of the world's best poetry brings us to a scenic lookout upon the plains of oneness, such as this quatrain of William Blake's: "To See a World in a Grain of Sand / And a Heaven in a Wild Flower / Hold Infinity in the palm of your hand / And Eternity in an hour."

However lyrical the words that come to us from this sublime consciousness, is it not too late for us to find ourselves and discover the All in this manner? We left that Garden of Eden a long time ago. Now we have a bad case of cramps after eating those apples of pride and egotism—by the bushel, no doubt, when the Industrial Revolution was gearing up. Yes, it is important to know when and how we lost that grace. What we need more immediately, however, is the emergence of a new knowledge. I don't think we can find it by cocking an ear to whispers from the past. Nor can we find it exclusively through our mind. Our mind is a function that, in propagandizing for our species' "superiority," we have misused and overrated. We need something that is revolutionary, a knowledge that penetrates the psyche the way we have penetrated the atom. We need to be humbled, to have our egotism split open, our negativity and passivity exposed and blown asunder, so that we *cannot* be put back together in the old form.

This knowledge can be summarized: *Through our unconscious negativity or emotional attachments, we place ourselves in a passive position vis-à-vis our inner aggression, which maintains its rule through this weakness of ours. This inner arrangement becomes the model for our relationship with others and for the culture and political society we create. Thus, our goal of greater freedom in this age of subtle tyranny is facilitated through the process of learning the secrets of our psyche.*

The hero's or heroine's journey to the land of true democracy is through the world of the psyche. The freedom we establish there is like a release from prison, followed by a coronation. Once we were compelled to entertain the negative, but now we can instead soak up pleasant, rich experiences. We are drawn to beauty. We take note of it and feel pleasure in our appreciation of it. We can feel gratitude for life as well as respect or love for whomever or whatever crosses our path. Being liberal or conservative is secondary. We can find pleasure in pondering infinity, marveling at the diversity of life, or wiggling our toes in the sand.

Will this growing ever stop? It feels like it can go on forever. We feel ourself expanding, while past and future converge into a timeless now. Our birth and our death fall in the same circle. The wholeness we are becoming extends into our democracy, into the universe, and into infinity.

Appendix

Variations on Our Unconscious Negativity

There are three primary categories of unconscious negativity, and they correspond with the three main stages of early childhood: The oral stage, the anal stage, and the genital stage. The amount of negativity with which an adult is burdened relates in part to how well as a child he navigated the shoals of his early emotional challenges.

In the oral stage, from birth to eighteen months, a child's primary experience is through the mucous membranes of the mouth. The child is conscious of oral satisfaction or oral deprivation. When his milk doesn't arrive when the child wants it or expects it, the child cries in protest. The child doesn't understand the relativity of time, so five or ten minutes can feel like forever to him. In his subjective, emotional inner world, the child begins to feel that he is being deprived or refused or *not getting*, and such feelings become an emotional stumbling block in his developing psyche. As adults, this negative expectation of *not getting* lingers in our psyche like a persistent virus or unresolved glitch and can include chronic feelings of being dissatisfied, impatient, entitled, and deprived. This issue fuels the buy-now, pay-later mentality of consumerism.

Variations on feeling deprived, refused, and *not getting* include expecting loss, never having enough, and never feeling satisfied. These underlying issues are a root cause of selfishness and greed.

The next stage, the anal stage, is experienced between eighteen months and thirty-six months. Now the child's awareness expands to take in his anal functions as he goes through the process of toilet training. This is the time of the "terrible two's," when children typically object to the process of toilet training. The experience can be quite unpleasant for children; they are aware that the parent's authority is being imposed on them and they resist having to comply.

The variations on feeling controlled include feeling trapped, dominated, restricted, inhibited, held up, made to endure inappropriate behavior, made to look bad, overwhelmed, and shamed. As adults, these unresolved negative emotions linger and can be seen in people who are controllers, procrastinators, obsessive-compulsives, and passive-aggressive manipulators. Unresolved anal issues are the problem for people who have trouble with bosses, who avoid intimacy because it feels like giving up one's power, or who appear to be easy-going and compliant but soon object to feeling controlled.

The third category of negative emotions originates in the genital stage, from two to four or five years of age. The child's consciousness has expanded from the sense of being just one, just himself, in the oral stage, to the sense of being two, himself and mother, in the anal stage, to finally being three, himself with mother and father, in the genital stage. Now the child becomes intensely interested in how he or she is being recognized, appreciated, and valued. On the negative side, the child is now quick to feel rejected, unloved, criticized, and unwanted.

Variations on these negative emotions include feeling insulted, humiliated, discounted, disrespected, and judged. In this stage, we often felt that we were not loved enough, or not in the right way, or that our siblings got more attention and validation. A child might have felt that his parents loved each other more than they loved him.

If this period is unresolved emotionally, we grow up to be adults with low self-esteem who can't represent ourselves effectively in the world. While inner passivity was taking shape inside us during the oral and anal stages, inner aggression is now forming in this genital stage, and our unconscious negativity now incorporates self-criticism, self-rejection, self-condemnation, and, in the extreme, self-hatred.

Common Consequences of Unconscious Negativity

Shame. Rather than admit to our readiness to be inwardly passive and to submit to the condemnation of inner aggression, we absorb the condemnation and consequently feel shame. It feels to us that shame is our problem, when the real problem is our absorption of aggression from the inner critic. Shame is the price we unconsciously agree to pay (based on what inner passivity, our weak inner defender, has negotiated on our behalf with inner aggression) to maintain the status quo and cover up our passive participation in the dialectic.

Anxiety. We feel anxious or fearful when we are being held accountable by the inner critic. The more inwardly passive we are, the more we live in worry, anxiety, fear, and even panic.

Boredom. This feeling is a result of our readiness to feel emotionally and visually deprived. What we have and what we see is not enough to satisfy us because of our emotional attachment to feeling deprived or refused. The unconscious negativity is our willingness to live in a state of deprivation, even at the price of chronic boredom.

Cravings. Whether for sex, food, money, or drugs, cravings can be associated with several negative attachments such as deprivation, control, and self-rejection. A person who is self-rejecting, for instance, can crave sexual partners because his connection to them feels at least temporarily like emotional acceptance or love. Typically, self-rejection, a form of inner aggression, is felt more painfully after such sexual encounters because the individual is chastised internally for debasing himself or herself.

Loneliness. Chronic loneliness results from the feeling that one's own person is insufficient or unworthy. The individual feels unloved and unwanted and doesn't realize his attachment to those feelings and his indulgence in them is creating his loneliness.

Guilt. As with shame, the person who frequently feels guilty is being accountable to the inner critic and allowing even the mild insinuations of such inner aggression to register like the pronouncements of a high court. Guilt is the concession offered by inner passivity to appease inner aggression.

Apathy. We can go numb to inner aggression, shrug our shoulders, and say we don't care, meaning we basically give up the fight and surrender. Inner aggression can't hurt us as much if we're numb. In adopting this defense, however, we have to become apathetic or depressed. We risk giving up on ourselves or being unable to emerge from the depths of this self-abandonment.

Exercises

The following exercises are designed to help individuals identify unconscious negativity. Because we are so well defended, we usually need professional help to identify our deep negativity and clear it out. However, not everyone can afford it, and often the help that is available does not address these deeper issues.

People who are committed enough can work the process described in this book through their acquisition of the knowledge and their effort with the exercises. Success would depend on one's persistence, patience, inner vigilance, and emotional health. Some of these exercises may overlap, in the sense that they seem to repeat similar steps and themes. This overlapping involves the process of coming at difficult-to-dislodge negativity from different angles.

Many of the suggestions and questions in these exercises can be addressed effectively by closing one's eyes and letting one's mind and feelings ramble over a thought or a scene for five or ten minutes or more. It's not necessary to think too hard. When we open our mind in the search for inner truth, significant memories and insight usually begin to emerge. Any reader who experiences significant emotional upset from these exercises should stop doing them and consult a mental-health counselor.

Parental Images

It is very helpful to develop a sense of how you experienced some of the emotional challenges of your childhood. This is done not to suffer in the present moment from painful memories, of course, but in order to understand more deeply the precise feelings that remain unresolved from your past. It is also done to support yourself, to see yourself in a heroic manner, as someone who has endured a lot to get to where you are now. Answer the following questions with whatever thoughts or feelings come to you, without thinking too much about it. When finished, answer the same questions substituting your father or guardians. (There is no point in rushing through an exercise; it can be done over several days.)

What kind of person was your mother?

How would you describe your relationship with her?

What was your mother's favorite saying about life?

How did she praise you? What did she say? How did she criticize you? What did she say?

When was she upset and how did she show it?

How did you react or respond when she was upset?

What were her expectations of you? How did she hope you would turn out?

What did your mother like most about you?

What did she dislike most about you?

How do you wish your mother might have been different?

What would you like from her? What did you need from her?

Be your mother right now. As your mother, how would you describe the son or daughter you are? Have her talk about the kind of relationship she had with you.

Make a list of all the strengths or positive qualities you see in your mother. Note how these are either manifested in you or in your cultivation of the opposite attributes. Try to be objective in seeing both your mother's strengths and your own.

Write a list of your mother's major weaknesses. Note how these are reflected in you, through acceptance or rejection of the traits. Be specific.

Write down the limitations in your life that you carry from your mother. How are you similar? Describe the pain and problems that are created for you by these limitations.

Make a statement that you feel uneasy or nervous about making that summarizes what you have always wanted to say to your mother about your experience of her. You wouldn't necessarily actually say this to your mother, of course. It is not necessary to involve your parents directly while working out your issues. Keep in mind that we usually are most similar in personality and temperament to the parent with whom we had the most difficulty.

Self-Imposed Put-Downs

Read each positive statement and reflect on it. Before going to the next statement, jot down as honestly as you can any negative comments that come to you. In other words, watch for the voices of your inner aggression and inner passivity. You can write this down or just make a note of it in your mind. Try to observe your dialectic of futility in action.

1. I am very pleased with myself.
2. I am a total success.
3. I have always been approved of and well liked by others.
4. I never worry about winning the approval of others.
5. I trust my ideas, perceptions, and opinions.
6. I have no difficulty making decisions and following through on them.
7. I only attract loving, positive people into my life.
8. I feel confident in expressing my feelings and having them acknowledged.
9. The expression of my intelligence and creativity helps and uplifts others.

Recognizing Transference

The purpose of this exercise is to understand how hurtful feelings or grievances from childhood are transferred onto present relationships or events. Whatever negative feelings we are attached to, we will experience them in our dealings with others. For instance, we often feel criticism or rejection from others even when they did not intend to criticize or reject us. Or we "see" ways in which we are convinced we are being deprived by others or by the world in general, when in fact we have many riches and blessings in our life.

1. Focus on how you are feeling in your life right now. How do you feel about yourself, what you are doing, and how you are relating to others? Describe your major emotional reactions.

2. Recall how you felt about yourself in your adolescent years (pick an age). What was happening and how did you feel? How do those feelings compare with the present?
3. Go back further and see yourself as a child (pick an age). Let your mind wander to some hurtful or disturbing childhood event. See yourself as that child and experience the feelings associated with that event. How did you feel and how did you react? How did you defend or protect yourself?
4. Ask yourself how in the present those old feelings affect your attitude toward life and other people? In what ways do you transfer those feelings onto people or circumstances in the present, experiencing again those unresolved negative emotions?
5. Describe how you may treat others or yourself in the manner you felt treated as a child by family members.
6. Reassure yourself that your temptation to experience the negative is ending for you, and that, through inner vigilance and knowledge, you are now determined to stop experiencing replays or variations of it in your life.

Owning our Unconscious Negativity

Owning this negativity is the first step in letting it go.

1. Describe the situation that is contributing to your emotional distress. Give the details of what is happening (or has happened) and how you are reacting (or reacted). What do you feel the

other person (or situation) is doing to you? For example, "He lectured me for an hour about how inadequate I am."

2. Now describe the feelings you experienced. It's easy to recognize the surface symptoms such as feeling angry, depressed, sad, fearful, or numb. However we want to go deeper. For example, "Yes I was angry because I felt rejected, discounted, and criticized." Or, "I was depressed because I felt cheated and deprived of what I want."
3. Go back into your childhood and recall an incident or incidents that bring up the same feelings. For example, who lectured you in your past? How did that feel?
4. Run through your life and recall how you have experienced those same feelings in different contexts and with different individuals. Note the prevalence of those feelings throughout your life.
5. We can take it a step further. Give examples of how you may have provoked the same reactions in others. For example, do you lecture others and criticize them in the same way that you were just lectured? The traits you despise in others are usually your own. If you feel that the other is withholding love, ask yourself, "How do I withhold love as well?" Remember that your success in this process depends on your being as honest as you can with yourself.
6. Describe how you subject yourself to the same treatment that you feel others subject you to. For example, how often do you lecture and criticize

yourself? How well do you support yourself and your position?

The Agony of Guilt

Guilt is the feeling that one deserves to be punished. Guilt is usually irrational, and it is commonly produced when we buy into (or give credence to) the irrational, mean-spirited insinuations and accusations of the inner critic. Guilt is felt for both our inner passivity and for the alleged transgression of which inner aggression accuses us.

Guilt is appropriate if you beat your spouse or rob a bank. But most of the time we feel guilty for minor or even nonexistent infractions. Guilty feelings disappear when we understand and work through the deeper issue. For instance, guilt is often the pound of flesh we offer up to cover up our passive indulgence in some form of our unconscious negativity. The following exercise can help identify how we use guilt as a defense.

1. List all the behaviors or actions that you feel guilty about.
2. Give examples of when other people have "laid" guilt trips on you. How did you react?
3. Give examples of the guilt trips you lay on yourself.
4. Give examples of guilt trips you have laid on others.
5. Give examples of guilt trips that your parents laid on you while you were growing up and later as an adult. Did you ever lay guilt trips on them, such

as trying to make them feel responsible for your feelings or life situation?

6. Try to become aware of what negative emotion hides behind your guilt. For instance, is your guilt a reaction to feeling rejected or criticized? If so, you are attached emotionally to feeling rejected or criticized, while, at the same time, this is the negative manner in which your inner aggression treats you.

Parental Patterns

As mentioned, many of us have a hard time remembering how we felt in our interactions with our parents and siblings. These feelings may be consciously forgotten but they remain in our unconscious, and they will surface in a disturbing, painful way when we unwittingly transfer these unresolved issues onto other people. It is liberating to understand how you interpreted your parents' behavior toward you and how you modeled yourself on their strengths and weaknesses.

By reconnecting with these old hurts and grievances, we become conscious of how we anticipate and promote these feelings in the present. Of course, the purpose is not to blame our problem on our parents or guardians, but to see and understand how we still play out being victims of their real or alleged malice or neglect.

1. Did your parents allow you to express your feelings openly or were you afraid to reveal what you thought or felt? Were you ever punished or made to feel bad for expressing these feelings? Are you afraid to express and reveal your feelings in

your personal relationships? What do you expect will happen if you do?

2. Describe the communication pattern in your family. Were verbal exchanges sarcastic, judgmental, superficial, nonexistent? Describe the quality of communication in your past and present relationships.
3. When you had a problem as a child, did your parents make it your fault, tease you, ridicule you, disapprove of you, protect you, ignore you, pamper you, make excuses for you, or dismiss you? Do you still experience these same feelings in your life? How and when?
4. Did your parents support your growing independence? Did they ask you questions about how you felt or perceived events? Did they allow you to participate in decisions affecting you? Or did you have to conform to their way of thinking and behaving? If you could go back to that time, what would you say to them, knowing what you know now? To what degree do you believe that you now act independently and autonomously?
5. Did your parents see you as a unique individual with needs and dreams? Did they recognize your talents? Or were you used to satisfy their needs and make them look good? Were you invisible to them? How has this affected your feelings about yourself and your ability to be expressive and creative in the present?
6. Did you ever feel unwanted by them? Or were you a source of delight to them? Do you have similar feelings with your friends and in relationships?

An example of the deep negative would be your continuing feeling, based on past experiences, that you are not appreciated or valued.

7. What measures did your parents use to control your behavior? Such measures could include threats, guilt, shame, intimidation, bribery, and sugary praise. Explore the same control measures in your present relationships. What is the effect for you and for others in relating to them in this way?
8. Were your parents able to admit their mistakes and take responsibility for their behaviors? Or did they deny any wrongdoing and blame others for their faults? Are you involved with someone else with the same problem? Explore the difficulty you might have in accepting criticism and admitting your mistakes.
9. Consider the extent to which you were praised and criticized by your parents. Did they put pressure on you to perform? How has their reaction to you affected your ability to perform in the present? Are you still reacting to their negative judgments? One common effect is for people to exhibit, often through failure in career and relationships, how they felt they were seen by their parents. Such self-sabotage can be reversed when the deep negative is exposed. Did interactions with your parents produce fear or guilt or a sense of well-being? Do you feel fear or guilt in your interactions with others?

Letting Go of Dislike for Others

Draw up a list of what you most dislike in others. Now consider how you possess these aspects in your unconscious (now becoming conscious) negativity. It is *projection* to see and dislike in others what you decline to see in yourself. In understanding projection, try to become aware of how determined we humans are *not* to see and become responsible for negativity in ourselves.

The Passive Wish

We can be very interested in framing our experience so that we feel passive. We might wake up in the morning and say with a big groan something to this effect, "I *have to* do the laundry, I *have to* go shopping, I *have to* mow the grass, and I *have to* take my pets to the vet." We are framing the experience in terms of our inner passivity, meaning we are feeling obligated or forced to do what are simply the requirements of daily life or we are feeling overwhelmed by our chores and duties. We are unconsciously making burdens of these requirements in order to live through our unresolved inner passivity.

Understanding the inner attraction for this negative experience helps you to refrain, for instance, from thinking about the coming day in terms of the effort it will require. If for some reason you are not looking forward to the day, then get up and try to take pleasure in the small things that the morning has to offer: A shower, a shave, a cup of coffee. The healthier you are, the more you feel a quiet pleasure in being present to yourself and cultivating inner peace as you prepare for or await coming challenges.

Fueling the Emotional Imagination

Our visual drive or emotional imagination can work against our best interests. Through unconscious negativity, the emotional imagination is always ready to create thoughts, feelings, beliefs, and scenarios that resurrect painful memories that are associated with suffering and self-defeating behaviors. If we don't intervene through our conscious self our experience of life and our capacity as citizens can be greatly diminished. The following exercise helps us understand how to acquire more self-regulation in this area.

1. Write down the most prominent negative scenarios you have recently experienced, been tempted to visualize, or conceivably been obsessed by. Examples include being killed in a car or airplane accident, starving in the gutter, being rejected by a lover or spouse, or being exposed as a fake or a fraud. To come up with these scenarios, it might help to ask yourself, "What have I been afraid of lately?"
2. Look into the memories of your childhood. Ask yourself, "Are any of my current fears similar to feelings I had in my childhood?" For example, the fear of being killed in a car accident could relate to a repressed feeling that your parents didn't care that much about you and your existence. Fear of flying can be a consequence of how, as a child, you didn't trust your parents. You might have felt they didn't support you emotionally, that they were going to let you down or not take care of you in some way. Remember that we can have good

or decent parents and still hold such irrational feelings. Now you have transferred that fear (the expectation of being let down) onto the pilot or onto the reliability of the airplane itself. Note in this case that, through your fear of flying, you are letting yourself down by not supporting yourself emotionally.

3. For each worst-case scenario you come up with, look for the bottom-line attachment, meaning your unconscious willingness to indulge in some old negative issue. Now you can begin to take responsibility for that negative feeling by seeing how you secretly maintain it and reinforce it through the misuse of your emotional imagination.

Finding the Middle

This exercise is designed to help establish a connection with your self and rise above the dialectic of futility.

1. List all the behaviors and patterns that you feel you have difficulty regulating. Examples would include overeating, drinking too much alcohol or coffee, inability to cut back on work hours, overspending, promiscuity, gambling, and so on. Let an image come that reflects the part of you that seems determined to continue with this behavior.
2. Have this part of you answer the following question: "I don't want to stop doing this because. . . . Next, list all the feelings and reasons this part gives for resisting moderation, for

instance: "It's too boring," or "I like the taste," or "I just want to do what I want to do."

3. Scan your memory to see if you can determine where this uncooperative part inside of you comes from. Was either of your parents involved with the same or similar unbalanced behavior, or did they manifest an opposite version of your behavior? For instance, if you are a workaholic, was your father lazy and irresponsible? Do this process for each behavior that you want to stop or moderate.
4. Now let an image come to you of another part in you that is critical or scornful of you for your unbalanced behavior. This part might be saying, *Why are you doing this to yourself? You're disgusting. You have no willpower! You're just a mush ball!* Write down the ways you reproach yourself for your feelings and behaviors.
5. Does this reproachful voice sound like your mother or father? Is it one of your siblings? The voice is coming from the inner critic, often as a caricature of a parental voice from childhood. Figuratively, take a step back, and observe the conflict that has been going on inside of you for some time now. Can you see how fruitless the conflict is? Realize that this conflict soaks up a great deal of your energy, while it also locks you into a limited, painful sense of yourself. Nonetheless, it is frightening to let this conflict go because you won't quite know who you are without it.
6. Imagine that a new part of you is emerging. This part does not associate itself with the critical part

nor with the passive part. This new part represents your self rising above the dialectic of futility. If you can't quite feel this part emerging, try to imagine what it would feel like if it did. Identify, define, and feel this new part as well as you can. Have this new part address both the weak, passive part and the critical part. What does it say to the weak part? To the critical part? Can it act as a mediator and take charge of the situation? What does that feel like? Or, how do you imagine that would feel?

The Observer in You

When you learn to observe your thoughts, fantasies, and emotional reactions without judgment, you have taken a big step toward regulating them. Take time out each day to chart the following:

1. Your thoughts and feelings about others. This includes: becoming aware of feeling their pain, trying to solve their problems, how you might confront them, what they think about you, what they have done to you or how they hurt you (in the past or present), analyzing their flaws, and considering how they have disappointed you.
2. Your thoughts and feelings about yourself. Do you engage in put-downs, reproaches, and other forms of self-criticism or self-derision? (Sometimes the quips or thoughts you make in this regard are instinctive and subtle.) Do you obsess on your past failures or blunders? Are you tempted to experience negative expectations about yourself

and your life, saying or feeling, for example, "I'll never amount to anything," or "What I think or feel doesn't matter."

3. Replays of past grievances and emotional injuries. Examples include the memory and feeling of not being invited to a party, a friend not calling you back, or other such "betrayals" experienced with friends, children, parents, or siblings. Such replays of old hurts mean you are sneaking into the deep negative for a hit on the feeling of being disrespected, criticized, rejected, or unloved.
4. Your daydreams. Are you concerned with what is going to happen in the future? This includes thoughts about impending catastrophes. What are your fears about the future? Do you reminisce on past glories? If overdone, you are looking for a way to feel helpless and passive in the present. When middle-aged men fantasize about being sports heroes they can be compensating for how their inner passivity leaves them feeling unfulfilled in the present.
5. A focus on lists or chores to be done. Do you have a drill-sergeant in your head? Are you preoccupied with not getting things done? One client made a list of all the things she wasn't accomplishing for the secret purpose of accentuating the pain of her entanglement in passivity.
6. The time you spend reflecting on feelings of deprivation, or control, or rejection. Catch yourself in the act of doing this. Catching it, you can snap your fingers and say, "Aha! I see what I'm doing. I got caught in the deep negative

> again. Thank goodness I understand this process now and see the compelling attraction of that particular negative attachment. I'm more vigilant and I'm starting to overcome this negative allure. I'm determined to succeed and I know I will."

The Highest Value

Contemplate the question: What is the highest value in your life? Is it having lots of money? Is it freedom from fear or suffering? Is it happiness? Is it love, truth, or joy? Is it the attainment of the fullest possible degree of wholeness? Whatever it is, imagine it happening. How would it feel to truly fulfill yourself? More importantly, how will you feel about yourself if it doesn't happen?

Embracing Your Aloneness

Close your eyes and try to quiet your mind. Allow yourself to approach the feeling of your aloneness. It might feel like a deep black hole of nothingness that you disappear into as your mind becomes silent. Is it frightening to do this? How much resistance comes up? Can you imagine your new witness self going eyeball-to-eyeball with the sense of nothingness and feeling at peace with it? If you can "hang out" with your nothingness for a while, you will begin to feel a sense of self that is not frightened or intimidated by the darkness within. Your self, as you get to know this indescribable you, is not afraid of life. It is a warrior's spirit and a lover's spirit and a spirit of democracy.

NOTES

[1] C.G. Jung. *The Undiscovered Self.* The New American Library. New York, 1958. pp. 105-106.

[2] George Lakoff. *don't think of an elephant! Know Your Values and Frame the Debate.* Chelsea Green Publishing. White River Junction, VT. 2004. pp. 16-30.

[3] Thomas Sowell. *A Conflict of Visions: Ideological Origins of Political Struggles.* Basic Books, NY. 2002. Sowell writes, "Inconsistent and hybrid visions make it impossible to equate constrained and unconstrained visions simply with the political left and right." p. 122. He also writes, "The unconstrained vision is clearly at home on the political left. . ." p. 124.

[4] A.H. Maslow. *The Farther Reaches of Human Nature.* Penguin Books, New York. 1976. p. 37.

[5] Lionel Trilling. *Sincerity and Authenticity.* Harvard University Press. Cambridge and London, 1971, 1972. p. 132.

[6] Erich Fromm. *The Sane Society.* Fawcett World Library. New York. 4th Printing. 1967. p. 314.

7 Ian Buruma. "The Indiscreet Charm of Tyranny." *The New York Review of Books.* May 12, 2005. p. 37.

8 *The Freud Reader.* Ed. Peter Gay. W.W. Norton & Co., New York, 1989. pp. 759-761.

9 Hendrik Hertzberg. *The New Yorker*, Aug. 11, 2003. p. 24.

10 José A. Argüelles. *The Transformative Vision.* Shambhala, Boulder & London. 1975. p. 203.

11 Literary critic Lionel Trilling, a student of psychoanalysis, offered an excellent understanding of the dialectic between the superego and the subordinate ego in *Sincerity and Authenticity*, from which the following is paraphrased and quoted: According to Freud, the superego or inner aggression was originally part of the ego but separated from it and established a position of authority over the ego and its activities. "We mistake the nature of the superego when we make it exactly synonymous, as we commonly do, with conscience. Only up to a point are the two coextensive. The operations of conscience are determined by its practical social intentions, but the superego is under no such limitation and in consequence its activity is anything but rational. The process it has instituted against the ego is largely gratuitous, beyond the needs of reason and beyond the reach of reason. The particular kind of pain it inflicts is that which Freud calls guilt [it also causes shame, anxiety, tension, depression, and fear]." Freud understood the formation of the superego to be a decisive

advance in the development of the mind. Through the superego, a form of self-regulation is internalized, and every person can now become a moral and social being, a supporter of civilization. Nonetheless, we cannot ignore the superego's "deplorable irrationality and cruelty." We face "the terrible paradox" through which the superego, while demanding renunciation on the part of the ego, increases its severity with that renunciation. "The aggression which the ego surrenders is appropriated by the superego to intensify its own aggression against the ego, an aggression which has no motive save that of its own aggrandizement." The "insatiable tyrant" does not confine its operations to the internal life of individuals. It "quickens and rationalizes man's rage against man." (Harvard University Press, 1971, 1972. pp. 150-155.)

[12] Lewis H. Lapham. "Tentacles of Rage: The Republican propaganda mill, a brief history." *Harper's Magazine.* September, 2004. p. 41.

[13] Ibid, p. 32.

[14] Ibid, p. 32.

[15] Eric Alterman. *What Liberal Media? The Truth about Bias and the News.* Basic Books, New York. 2003. pp. 245-256.

[16] John Luckacs. *At The End of An Age.* Yale University Press, New Haven and London. 2002. pp. 176-177.

[17] Lance Morrow. *Evil: An Investigation*. Basic Books, New York. p. 50.

[18] John Horgan. "Can Science Explain Consciousness?" *The Scientific American Book of the Brain.* The Lyons Press, Guilford, CT. 1999. p. 302.

[19] The idea that we are psychologically attached to negative emotions was developed by a psychoanalyst named Edmund Bergler (1900-1962). Bergler wrote twenty-three psychology books (some released by major New York publishers) and 273 published articles, and a 400-word obituary was written about him in *The New York Times.* His latest book, *The Talent for Stupidity: The Psychology of the Bungler, the Incompetent, and the Ineffectual,* was published in 1998, thirty-six years after his death, by International Universities Press in Madison, CT, which still has many of his titles in print. Bergler is not widely known or studied, and his contention that homosexuality is a neurotic disorder makes him appear dated and irrelevant, though his writings on homosexuality can be read in the context of mid-Twentieth Century attitudes and are a small part of his prodigious output. He was aware of the enormous resistance to his theory about emotional attachments, and he certainly understood how determined we are, through our defenses, not to disturb the psychic status quo. He once said his books were time-bombs that would go off in 100 years. Perhaps now, faced in these critical times with the need to break out of our personal and national malaise, we can speed up the timetable.

[20] Antonio Damasio. *Looking for Spinoza: Joy, Sorrow, and the Feeling Brain.* Harcourt, Inc. New York, 2003. p. 131.

[21] John J. Ratey, M.D. *A User's Guide to the Brain.* Vintage Books. New York, 2001. p. 144.

[22] Peter Gay. *Reading Freud: Explorations and Entertainments.* Yale University Press. New Haven & London. 1990. p. 93.

[23] Jacob Needleman. *The American Soul: Rediscovering the Wisdom of the Founders.* Jeremy P. Tarcher / Putnam, New York. 2003. p. xx.

[24] Wendell Berry. *Citizenship Papers.* Shoemaker & Hoard. Washington, DC. 2003. p. 87.

[25] Alan Taylor. "Midnight Ramblers." *The New Republic.* Feb. 5, 2001. p. 40.

[26] Eric Foner. *The Story of American Freedom.* W.W. Norton and Co., New York. 1998. p. 4.

[27] Harold Bloom. *How to Read and Why.* Scribner, New York. 2000. p. 22.

[28] Harold Bloom. *Shakespeare: The Invention of the Human.* Penguin Putnam Inc., New York. 1998. p. 269.

[29] "Nothingness." *Parabola*, New York. Summer, 2000. p. 59-61.

[30] Robert Ellwood. *Theosophy: A modern expression of the wisdom of the ages.* Theosophical Publishing House, Wheaton, IL. 1986. p. 23.

[31] Robert Jay Lifton. *Superpower Syndrome: America's Apocalyptic Confrontation with the World.* Thunder Mouth Press / Nation Books, New York. 2003. p. 3.

[32] Andrew Harvey. *The Essential Mystics: The Soul's Journey into Truth.* Castle Books, Edison, NJ. 1998. p. 1.

[33] *Ibid.* p. 4.

About the Author

Peter Michaelson is a psychotherapist in private practice in Santa Fe, New Mexico. He is a former journalist and science writer, and can be reached through his websites at www.QuestForSelf.com and www.PeterMichaelson.com.

Printed in the United States
78717LV00001B/29

9 781425 912185